P9-DEV-332

# The Pocket DJ

**Ultragrrrl's guide to building the best music library >>>>>>**

## By Sarah Lewitinn

**SIMON SPOTLIGHT ENTERTAINMENT**
New York  London  Toronto  Sydney

**SIMON SPOTLIGHT ENTERTAINMENT**

An imprint of Simon & Schuster

1230 Avenue of the Americas, New York, New York 10020

Text copyright © 2005 by Sarah Lewitinn

SIMON SPOTLIGHT ENTERTAINMENT and related logo are trademarks
of Simon & Schuster, Inc.

Manufactured in the United States of America

First Edition 10 9 8 7 6 5 4 3 2 1

Library of Congress Cataloging-in-Publication Data

Lewitinn, Sarah.

The pocket DJ / by Sarah Lewitinn.— 1st ed.

p. cm.

ISBN-13: 978-1-4169-0723-7 (alk. paper)

ISBN-10: 1-4169-0723-8 (alk. paper)

1. Disc jockeys—Vocational guidance. I. Title.

ML3795.L4 2005

781.64—dc22

2005012092

## ACKNOWLEDGMENTS

First and foremost, thank you to my big brother Lawrence for giving me his amazing vinyl collection, for turning me on to good music, and for convincing Mom and Dad that I wasn't up to no good. Without you, this book would not have been possible. Thanks to Mom and Dad for making me and for letting me listen to my music in the car every once in a while, my brother Albert for letting me live with him for free for two years, and my beloved, dearly departed Maxine. Thanks to my wonderful editor Tricia Boczkowski at the wonderful Simon Spotlight Entertainment; my agent, Jim Fitzgerald; and my lawyer, Vivien Lewitt. I would also like to thank Karen Ruttner, Josh Madden, Brian Battjer, and Niki Kanodia for their patience, friendship, love, and acceptance of me even when I'm the most embarrassing friend to have; my roommates Elizabeth Goodman, Sarah Wilson, Lindsay Robertson, and Gurj Bassi, who all made sure

I wasn't dead many times in the past; Marc Spitz for teaching me how to spin vinyl and being my mentor; Rob Stevenson for being the best; Alex English, Neil, and Lasse for throwing my first parties with me; Dalia for liking Nirvana; Mikey Way for being my first boyfriend; all my other boyfriends; Victoria DeSilverio for being a partner in crime for so long; the Killers (and Wyatt and Braden) for being the family from Las Vegas that I never had; Interpol for blowing my mind over and over again with such gorgeous music and not minding my slight obsession.

And thank you to: Mark, Greg, and Ollie of the Oohlas; Amy Chance; Shaun Lopez; Andy Greenwald; Nancy, Maurice, Eric, Elliot, and Renee Tabache; the Didias; Joel Madden; Rob Hitt; Brandon Flowers; Ronnie Vannucci; Carlos D; Simon LeBon; Joy Division; New Order; Mary-Kate Olsen; Kaiser Chiefs; Jenny Eliscu; Chuck Klosterman; Junior Sanchez; Gideon Yago; Greg Johnson; Raphael Rodriguez; Antony Ellis; James Iha; Ben Lee; Senses Fail; Joakim Ahlund and the

Caesars; Matt Rubano; Stephen Chbosky; Saints+Lovers; Joe Cardamone; Elhaam; Jenny Verdon; Ben Epstein; Matt Devine; Daniel Davis; Ellen Hart; John Fewell; MC Chris; Greg Smeck; Bruce Gainsford (for . . . you know what); Sia Michel; Michael Hirschorn; Laura Young; Lyor Cohen; Fred Feldman; Kenny W; Jason Roth; Heidi at Girlie; Leslie Simon; Roddy Woomble; Sheal; Alex Chow; Josh Zucker; Ryan Rayhill; Greg, Leigh, and Geo of the MisShapes; Thomas Onorato; Sean Dak; Jordan Silver; Imran Ahmed; Tom Ellis; Kimberly Taylor-Bennett; Dave Caggilari; Tim Vigorn; Anthony Shaw; Stephen Jones; Barry Nicholson; Steve Aoki; Steve Feinberg; Sydney Rose; Allison Mann; the Undesireables; Tenafly, NJ; Catrinel; Meredith Silverman; Jasper Coolidge; Audrey Levy; Scott Lapatine; Mark Grambo; Trent, Mike Palan, and every other blogger who makes me waste my day; Hardcore Dave Fisher; Max Bernstein; Julie Pietrangelo and Brian Reynolds; Caryn Ganz; Phoebe Reilly; Jake Hill; Elaine Garza; Tracey Pepper; Doug Brod; Charles Aaron; Daniela

Jung; Barbara Lang; Jennifer Frommer; Maureen Callahan; Alan Light; Jason Moore; Doug Purkel; Marti Zimlin; Dan Marcus; Adi Eliyahu; Adam Mandel; Josh Fontaine; Ed Lim; Mark Cheney; Dan Perrone; Peter Gaston; Cedric Lemoyne; Chris Kelly; Colleen Flood; Iann Robinson; Jake Fogelnest; Jason Hill; Jocelyn Malheiro; Johnny Kaps; Ridge Rooms; Brandon Reilly; Joe McCaffrey; and Travis Keller.

I would like to thank the following bands for ruling: My Chemical Romance, the Killers, the Oohlas, Muse, Interpol, Radiohead, the Smiths, Morrissey, Blur, Oasis, Primal Scream, Joy Division, Beck, Hole, Nirvana, the Spinto Band, and Arcade Fire.

# >> CONTENTS >>

# INTRODUCTION

**Music. Nothing, apart from religion perhaps, has the same ability to unite different people. Maybe that's why, to many of us, it's just that—it's what we believe in and what matters the most to us. I'm one of those people.**

One of my earliest music memories occurred when I was eight years old and on vacation with my mother and my brother Lawrence. We were in France, and for some reason we had walked into an electronics store with giant television sets. Playing on the big screens throughout the store was a live performance video of Michael Jackson's. I had gotten into his music through my best friend, Alexis Levy, who was also a die-hard George Michael fan. (Her gorgeous mom used to lead us in singing along to "I Want Your Sex" and "Monkey.") As usual, my brother had to come find me after I had strayed away. He discovered me dancing and singing my heart out in front of the TVs and nearly had a heart attack.

"Michael Jackson sucks!" he yelled. "You need to listen to better music." He then stuck his cheap Walkman in my little hands and said, "Listen to this."

Inside was a Pet Shop Boys tape. I don't really remember anything else about that trip, yet this particular moment with my brother changed my life.

Lawrence's room was next to mine, and while growing up I would constantly hear Echo & the Bunnymen, New Order, and Joy Division leaking through the walls. Sometimes I'd stick my ear against his door to hear the music better. (He was in high school at the time and going through his rebellious phase, so he didn't like having me around.) Meanwhile, across the hall was my brother Albert's room, and from there I could hear Madonna blasting. I had a better relationship with Albert at the time, and I remember hanging out in his room as we danced around to "Vogue" and other Top 40 hits.

Down the hall was my parents' room. Egyptian-Jewish refugees, they were big on the Arabic songs of their youth. My mom would drive me around in her car, and the only thing she'd want to listen to was the tunes from her homeland. Listening to her music taught me a little bit of Arabic (which will be useful should I ever need to say, "I love you, my darling—hurry to me"), if nothing else.

These different influences early in my life as a music listener taught me to be open-minded about everything I listened to. I got into music as an eight-year-old who didn't know the difference between Top 40 and alternative. I liked whatever made me feel something inside, be it happiness, sadness, or excitement.

Being open-minded as a music listener is the first step you need to take when reading this book. It's not for the snobby or elitist. It's not for people who aren't willing to give things they don't know—or are prejudiced against—a shot. It's for people who have digital music players and want to have the best fucking songs at their fingertips, without boundaries. It's for people who want to be able to create a soundtrack to their days. It's for people who want to be reminded of songs they've forgotten and learn about the ones they never knew about. It's about enjoying life.

This book is by no means the definitive guide to music. It's an introduction for people who are starting to get into it and a helpful reference guide for those who are already well on their way to being music heads.

One thing I've discovered is that we're all DJs in our own way. There are misconceptions about what a DJ is, but there are two basic qualities that all DJs share: They are technically skilled at blending one song into another in a way that makes everything flow smoothly without missing a beat, and they know how to pick the right songs for the right occasion. What good is being amazing at mixing if you're playing songs that aren't really appropriate for the moment? It doesn't matter if that moment is at a superclub in New York

City, London, Los Angeles, Paris, or Ibiza, or at a dingy bar in a small town, or while entertaining a bunch of friends at your house, or while doing the dishes. It's about playing the right song.

You can do it! I know you can. Anyone can. I'll show you how, right here, in this book. Not only will you get tips for the best songs to play at any time (literally, *any* time) and essential songs by artists you should know to open your musical horizons, but you'll also get tips on how to become a DJ who gets heard by others. In addition, you'll get suggestions for mixes you can make for your friends, tips on utilizing your digital music player (DMP) and its playlist functions, the scoop on what notable music-industry people are listening to, ideas about gadgets to pimp out your DMP, and a guide to finding music online. All in this tiny little book!

As the great songwriter George Michael once said: *Listen without prejudice.*

# TOOLBOX

## WHAT YOU NEED

If you want to be a DJ, be it in your home or out on the scene, there are a few things you will need to get started:

>**Music**

>**Music player**

>**Equipment**

## MUSIC

Times have changed. No longer is it considered lame to DJ with CDs or even an iPod. Vinyl is not only hard to come by for some of today's popular songs, but it can also be heavy and hard to transport from place to place. When I first started out DJing, I used both vinyl and CDs. But at the end of a night of lugging it around, I would get very discouraged by how hard it was to carry a bag of fifty records home after a party. I eventually realized that it was time I bit the bullet and switched over to something more compatible with my busy schedule, which kept me running around from party to party. These days, many of my peers are doing the same. Anyone who discourages this practice needs to be ignored.

Basically what I'm saying is that you don't need to go record hunting for hours on end, depleting your bank account, just because some jerk looks at you funny when you press play on a CD deck instead of putting a needle on a record. Not only that, but it's really easy to find the most obscure songs on the Net. It's easy and affordable (if not offered free of charge on occasion), and in about ten hours you can have a music library that took me years to cultivate.

The cool thing about digital music is that you can always add music to your library as time goes on. For instance, I generally DJ indie-rock dance parties, so I keep two copies of my Indie Dance Party playlist with me at all times.

I use that as the basis of my set and then I mix in several other discs filled with music that just came out, remixes of songs I already know will be crowd pleasers, or different tracks from those that are usually played by a certain artist. I also bring other playlists that are outside of the genre I intend to play that night. Hip-Hop/R & B Cheesy Dance Party always works well, as does anything from New Wave.

Being a DJ means knowing what music to play.

I invite you to use *The Pocket DJ* like a cookbook—you can follow the playlist recipes exactly or adapt them to suit your particular tastes. You'll find songs you know and love but don't have, suggestions for new music you might want to check out, and methods for organizing all of it into handy playlists to suit any mood. Mainly, I hope it inspires you to download good music.

## MUSIC PLAYER

As I mentioned above, you can DJ from CDs as well as from digital music players. If you intend to try your hand at DJing without turntables, you will need to use either a digital music player *and* CDs or two digital music players so you can go from song to song without having dead air in between. ("Dead air" is that break between songs when no music is playing. When you're DJing, you never want this to happen.) Obviously, if you're just playing tunes in a casual setting, there's no need to worry about any of this. Just press play, sit back, and chill out.

## EQUIPMENT

Here is the equipment you will need when you are DJing:

**>CDs and/or digital music player**

**>Headphones and an adapter for your head-phones that fits a ⅛" stereo plug to a ¼" stereo jack. This will make your regular headphones fit into most mixers.**

>The proper wires that go from your CD decks/DMP into your mixer. If you are DJing with a DMP, bring your own adapter cables. Not many clubs are equipped with them. You'll want to get an audio Y-splitter cable (3.5 mm plug for two RCA jacks). It's basically a headphone jack that plugs into the back of your DMP, attached to two "male" jacks that plug into the back of a mixer or stereo. This is what it looks like:

# HOW TO BE A DJ
# IN A FEW EASY STEPS

There are a bunch of great reasons to be a DJ, the best being that music is awesome and you want to hear songs you think are fantastic really loudly while enriching other people's lives at the same time. Ever go to a party where everyone is dancing and forgetting all their worries? It's the most amazing thing ever. To "lose yourself in the music, the moment," as Eminem has said, relieves stress, is great exercise, and can bring people closer together, literally.

Another great reason is that the money can be ridiculously good. Club DJs can make anywhere from fifty to a thousand dollars an hour for playing music. Sure, the more technically skilled you are, the more in demand you become, and the more money you can demand for your appearances. But getting fifty dollars an hour to play stuff you'd be listening to at home anyway is pretty cool.

Anyone can do it. I've taught people how to be a decent enough DJ (i.e., how to press play on a CD deck at precisely the right moment) in the span of ten minutes. I'm waiting to encounter a monkey with good music taste to prove my theory that DJing is so easy that even a monkey can do it. I realize that I might be insulting the "real" DJs who mix, beat match, and do all those fancy things, but I'm assuming they'll skip this chapter anyway.

## KNOW WHAT KIND OF MUSIC YOU WANT TO PLAY

Do you want to be a hip-hop DJ? A rock DJ? An eighties-music DJ? Figure that out and gather your songs and albums together; you can look through this book for surefire songs that will be a hit for whatever genre you pick. A typical set is about an hour long and should never consist of repeats by the same artist. (Note that some of the playlists in this book do repeat artists, but that's just because some songs are too good to leave out.) Also, don't hesitate to include songs that aren't in your genre but are kind of fun. If you're doing a set that's mostly new wave and you suddenly drop a popular hip-hop song, you'll be surprised how effectively it will reenergize the room.

## DJ YOUR FRIEND'S HOUSE PARTY

DJing a friend's house party is a great way to cut your teeth before trying out your set on a crowded bar or club. It's a good confidence-builder and gives you a chance to test out your new equipment (see page 9) in a casual environment among friends. If you live in a town where there aren't many bars you like, or if you're too young to be going to bars, then DJing house parties is a good option. After all, you've got to start somewhere.

## FIND A BAR OR CLUB TO DJ

I started out as a DJ promoter before I became a club DJ. A bar or club that isn't getting that much business (but is a decent enough joint that your friends wouldn't mind hanging out there) would be thrilled if you asked if you could throw a party there and supply the DJs. Just make sure that the place is set up with decks, a monitor, amps, and so on so you can do your thing.

The next step is getting people to come hear you spin. I suggest finding a friend who is about to have a birthday and centering the party on this event. That way a lot of people are guaranteed to come, and the owner of the venue will be impressed by your ability to draw a crowd, which is really his or her biggest concern. Remember, you are doing the owner a favor by bringing a thirsty crowd, so don't offer to pay any money for use of the place. Just call ahead and talk to the manager about reserving a night.

Okay, so you throw a birthday party and tons of people come and a bar that normally doesn't do too well on that particular night of the week is packed and selling booze like crazy. This is the perfect opportunity to tell the manager that you want to throw a weekly or monthly party. (I suggest doing a monthly to begin with, since it'll be easier for you to get people to come to a party that only happens once a month.) Tell him you want ten percent of the bar take after a set guarantee (the sum you guarantee the bar will make the night of your party). Guarantees range from five hundred to two thousand dollars, depending on what city you're in. But save the negotiations for later—these points can be discussed over the phone once the initial inquiries are out of the way.

To ensure a crowd every time, I suggest that you get different people to DJ an hour-long set with you at every party. Figure that if you bring four people to DJ and each person brings ten friends, you've got forty people right there in addition to your regular crew. See if you can get a DJ budget from the manager of the bar; otherwise, offer the other DJs a cut of your bar earnings. Let them know that the more money people spend at the bar, the more money will land in their pockets.

## HOW TO DJ USING CDS

All right, so you've got your music together—your albums and mix CDs. If you have a mix CD that has all the perfect songs for a DJ set, make two copies of it. In most settings you will have three things in front of you: two disc players and one mixer. Now here is what you do, in the most basic terms possible:

**1. Turn down the volume on both CDs. The volume controls are the large knobs on the mixer that slide up and down.**

**2. Press the cue button above the volume-control knob for one of the CD decks. This allows you to hear what is playing on that CD deck through your headphones.**

**3. Press play on the CD deck and choose the song you want to play.**

**4. Select the song, listen to it, and determine what the best way to go into the song is. Some songs begin right away. If this is the case, press pause on the song and press the track-rewind button to go back to the beginning of the track. Then raise the volume control on the mixer and press play.**

**5.** Once you have that song playing, press the same cue button again. Then press the other cue button to hear that CD deck.

**6.** Repeat step 4. If the song doesn't begin right away, you're going to want to mix it in. This means beginning the song on the second CD deck before the song on the first one is complete. Slowly raise the volume on the second CD deck while slowly lowering the volume on the first one.

**7.** Repeat these steps.

TA-DA! I told you it was easy!

## >> ESSENTIAL GENRES >>

## MENU

## >> ESSENTIAL GENRES >>

Sometimes when you're getting into music, you just don't know where to start. You think, "All right, that song I just heard seemed really cool, but I don't know where to go from there." It's okay! I did the work for you! This isn't the definitive guide to any genre, but it's a good start. These lists reflect what I feel are the essential songs to help you get your foot in the door of music. These are the songs that, as a DJ, you should probably have in your collection, because one day, someone is going to come up to you while you're doing your thing on the decks and say, "Could you play 'Gonna Make You Sweat (Everybody Dance Now),' please?" And you'll be able to say, "Of course!" or "No! Leave me alone! Read the sign! No requests!" And then you can, like, totally aggressively turn your body around, huff, and then stick that shit on and be like, "EVERYBODY DANCE NOW!" If, as a DJ, you take any of my advice at all, please take this one piece based on experience: Always have a hip-hop mix with you. ALWAYS. People will always ask for more hip-hop.

## 50s DANCE SONGS

The world was introduced to rock 'n' roll for the first time in the fifties, and amazingly, the songs still hold up as some of the greatest rock songs of all time. There's a reason why they're considered classics.

ESSENTIAL GENRES

01 **Bill Haley and His Comets** - Rock Around the Clock
02 **Chuck Berry** - Johnny B. Goode
03 **Jerry Lee Lewis** - Whole Lotta Shakin' Goin' On
04 **Ricky Nelson** - Hello Mary Lou
05 **Connie Francis** - Who's Sorry Now?
06 **Danny and the Juniors** - At the Hop
07 **Ritchie Valens** - *La Bamba*
08 **Elvis Presley** - Jailhouse Rock
09 **Little Richard** - Good Golly, Miss Molly
10 **The Diamonds** - The Stroll
11 **The Everly Brothers** - Wake Up Little Susie
12 **The Big Bopper** - Chantilly Lace
13 **Frankie Lymon and the Teenagers** - Why Do Fools Fall in Love?
14 **The Coasters** - Yakety Yak
15 **The Champs** - Tequila

16 **Little Richard** - Tutti Frutti
17 **Connie Francis** - Lipstick on Your Collar
18 **Chuck Berry** - Sweet Little Sixteen
19 **Jackie Wilson** - Lonely Teardrops
20 **Buddy Holly and the Crickets** - That'll Be the Day
21 **Ricky Nelson** - Believe What You Say
22 **Fats Domino** - Blueberry Hill
23 **Big Joe Turner** - Shake, Rattle & Roll
24 **Elvis Presley** - Hound Dog
25 **Jerry Lee Lewis** - Great Balls of Fire
26 **Santo & Johnny** - Sleep Walk

ESSENTIAL GENRES

## 60s DANCE SONGS

The sixties bridged the gap between the innocence of the fifties and the drug fueled decadence of the seventies. This decade also happened to produce some of the most fun soul and R & B classics.

01 **The Beatles** - Twist and Shout
02 **Aretha Franklin** - Respect
03 **Sam the Sham & the Pharaohs** - Wooly Bully
04 **Dusty Springfield** - Son of a Preacher Man
05 **Fontella Bass** - Rescue Me
06 **James Brown** - Papa's Got a Brand New Bag
07 **The Rolling Stones** - (I Can't Get No) Satisfaction
08 **The Turtles** - Happy Together
09 **Sam and Dave** - Soul Man
10 **Strawberry Alarm Clock** - Incense and Peppermints
11 **Tommy James & the Shondells** - I Think We're Alone Now*
12 **The Beach Boys** - I Get Around
13 **The Righteous Brothers** - You've Lost That Lovin' Feelin'
14 **Sonny & Cher** - I Got You Babe**

23

15 **The Drifters** - Under the Boardwalk

16 **The Shangri-Las** - Leader of the Pack

17 **The Temptations** - My Girl

18 **The Supremes** - Stop! In the Name of Love

19 **Lesley Gore** - It's My Party

20 **The Kingsmen** - Louie Louie

21 **The Angels** - My Boyfriend's Back

22 **Little Eva** - The Loco-Motion

23 **Del Shannon** - Runaway

24 **Dion** - Runaround Sue

25 **The Shirelles** - Will You Love Me Tomorrow

26 **Chubby Checker** - The Twist

27 **The Monkees** - I'm a Believer***

28 **The Lovin' Spoonful** - Summer in the City

29 **The Troggs** - Wild Thing

30 **The Lemon Pipers** - Green Tambourine

31 **Ohio Express** - Yummy Yummy Yummy

32 **The 5th Dimension** - Aquarius/Let the Sunshine In

33 **The Archies** - Sugar, Sugar

34 **Tommy James & the Shondells** - Crimson & Clover

35 **Marvin Gaye** - I Heard It Through the Grapevine

36 **The Mamas & the Papas** - California Dreamin'

ESSENTIAL GENRES

37 **The Dixie Cups** - Chapel of Love

38 **The Beach Boys** - Surfin' Safari

39 **Martha & the Vandellas** - (Love Is Like a) Heat Wave

40 **Isley Brothers** - Twist and Shout

41 **Van Morrison** - Brown Eyed Girl

42 **The Bobby Fuller Four** - I Fought the Law\*\*\*\*

43 **Creedence Clearwater Revival** - Proud Mary

\*      Covered (in the eighties) by teen pop star Tiffany

\*\*     In the nineties, Cher remade this song with cartoon characters Beavis and Butt-head for the film *Beavis and Butt-head Do America*.

\*\*\*    Interesting fact: This song was written by Neil Diamond.

\*\*\*\* This song became a signature tune for the British punk band the Clash in the seventies.

## 70s DANCE SONGS

The seventies was the breeding ground for two genres of music that couldn't be more different, but are both incredibly danceable: disco and punk.

01 **Chic** - Le Freak
02 **Iggy Pop** - Lust for Life
03 **The Jackson 5** - I Want You Back
04 **Shirley Ellis** - The Clapping Song
05 **The Runaways** - Cherry Bomb
06 **KC and The Sunshine Band** - Get Down Tonight
07 **Leo Sayer** - You Make Me Feel Like Dancing
08 **Wild Cherry** - Play That Funky Music
09 **Bay City Rollers** - Saturday Night
10 **Yvonne Elliman** - If I Can't Have You
11 **Joy Division** - Love Will Tear Us Apart*
12 **Blondie** - Heart of Glass**
13 **The Knack** - My Sharona
14 **Gloria Gaynor** - I Will Survive
15 **New York Dolls** - Personality Crisis
16 **Village People** - Y.M.C.A.
17 **Anita Ward** - Ring My Bell
18 **Buzzcocks** - What Do I Get?
19 **Kool & the Gang** - Celebration

20 **Sister Sledge** - We Are Family
21 **Ike and Tina Turner** - Proud Mary
22 **Talking Heads** - Psycho Killer
23 **Hot Chocolate** - You Sexy Thing
24 **Patti LaBelle** - Lady Marmalade
25 **Johnny Rivers** - Help Me, Rhonda
26 **Carl Douglas** - Kung Fu Fighting
27 **Blue Öyster Cult** - (Don't Fear) The Reaper
28 **Ramones** - Blitzkrieg Bop
29 **The Jam** - In the City
30 **The Undertones** - Teenage Kicks

ESSENTIAL GENRES

---

\*    Joy Division's lead singer, Ian Curtis, killed himself just before the British band was to start its first ever American tour. The remaining members of Joy Division went on to form New Order.

\*\*   This was considered a groundbreaking song, as Blondie was one of the first punk bands to embrace disco.

## 70s SOUNDTRACK SONGS

Picture this: You're hanging out, minding your own business, and then suddenly a song from *Saturday Night Fever* comes on and you're reliving a memory that isn't even yours, your finger darting diagonally from side to side. Next thing you know, you're remembering what it was like to be a black cop. Oh, the wonderful ways soundtracks help us relive our happiest memories.

01 **Carly Simon** - Nobody Does It Better (*The Spy Who Loved Me*)
02 **Richard O'Brien** - The Time Warp (*The Rocky Horror Picture Show*)
03 **Mick Jagger** - Memo From Turner (*Performance*)
04 **Nino Rota** - Godfather Waltz (*The Godfather*)
05 **Cheap Trick** - Surrender (*Over the Edge*)
06 **Cat Stevens** - If You Want to Sing Out, Sing Out (*Harold and Maude*)
07 **The Muppets** - The Rainbow Connection (*The Muppet Movie*)
08 **Curtis Mayfield** - Freddie's Dead (*Superfly*)
09 **Meco** - *Star Wars* Theme/Cantina Band (*Star Wars*)
10 **John Travolta/Olivia Newton-John** -

Summer Nights (*Grease*)

11 **Mike Oldfield** - Tubular Bells (*The Exorcist*)

12 **Bee Gees** - Night Fever (*Saturday Night Fever*)

13 **Isaac Hayes** - Theme from *Shaft* (*Shaft*)

14 **The Carrie Nations** - Come With the Gentle People (*Beyond the Valley of the Dolls*)

15 **Bobby Womack** - Across 110th Street (*Across 110th Street*)

16 **Walter Carlos** - Theme From *A Clockwork Orange* (Beethoviana) (*A Clockwork Orange*)

17 **Lalo Schifrin** - Broken Mirrors (*Enter the Dragon*)

18 **Joe Walsh** - In the City (*The Warriors*)

19 **Lloyd Williams** - Shout (*Animal House*)\*

20 **Barbra Steisand** - Evergreen (*A Star Is Born*)

21 **Sid Vicious** - My Way (*The Great Rock 'N' Roll Swindle*)

22 **John Williams** - Main Title (Theme from *Jaws*) (*Jaws*)

23 **Archie Hahn** - Goodbye, Eddie, Goodbye (*Phantom of the Paradise*)

24 **Earth, Wind & Fire** - Got to Get You Into My Life (*Sgt. Pepper's Lonely Hearts Club Band*)

25 **Maureen McGovern** - The Morning After (*The Poseidon Adventure*)

---

\*    Otis Day and the Nights lip-synched this song in the movie.

ESSENTIAL GENRES

## 80s DANCE SONGS

With MTV on the air, bands finally got to showcase the thing that mattered the most to them: their looks. No, but seriously, MTV really loved to play new-wave bands and hair-metal bands, throwing in some teeny pop in between. Kind of like this mix . . .

01 **a-ha** - Take On Me
02 **Toni Basil** - Mickey
03 **Warrant** - Cherry Pie*
04 **The Buggles** - Video Killed the Radio Star
05 **Scorpions** - Rock You Like a Hurricane
06 **The Bangles** - Walk Like an Egyptian
07 **Falco** - Rock Me Amadeus
08 **Eurythmics** - Sweet Dreams (Are Made of This)
09 **Quiet Riot** - Cum On Feel the Noize
10 **Tiffany** - I Think We're Alone Now
11 **Katrina and the Waves** - Walking On Sunshine
12 **The Fixx** - One Thing Leads to Another
13 **Wham!** - Wake Me Up Before You Go-Go
14 **Duran Duran** - Hungry Like the Wolf
15 **Guns N' Roses** - Welcome to the Jungle
16 **Pat Benatar** - Love Is a Battlefield
17 **New Kids on the Block** - Hangin' Tough

18 **Corey Hart** - Sunglasses at Night

19 **Culture Club** - Karma Chameleon

20 **Soft Cell** - Tainted Love

21 **Men Without Hats** - Safety Dance

22 **After the Fire** - Der Kommissar

23 **Billy Idol** - Dancing With Myself**

24 **Whitesnake** - Here I Go Again

25 **Nena** - *99 Luftballons*

26 **Robert Palmer** - Addicted to Love

27 **Frankie Goes to Hollywood** - Relax

28 **Cyndi Lauper** - She Bop***

29 **Kajagoogoo** - Too Shy

30 **Dexys Midnight Runners** - Come On Eileen

31 **Rick Springfield** - Jessie's Girl

32 **Madness** - Our House

33 **Thompson Twins** - Hold Me Now

ESSENTIAL GENRES

---

\*     Technically, this song came out in 1990, but it sounds pretty eighties to me.

\*\*    This song is about masturbation!

\*\*\* So is this one!

## 80s SOUNDTRACK SONGS

If you're like me, eighties movies were not only a favorite, they were a necessity in your life. You remember exactly what was playing when Lloyd Dobbler was holding his boom box above his head while standing under Diane Cort's window, and to this day whenever you hear "Tequila" you want to start dancing like Pee-Wee Herman. Well, here's a refresher for other great songs that will have you falling in love again.

01 **Bill Medley and Jennifer Warnes** - (I've Had) The Time of My Life (*Dirty Dancing*)

02 **Patrick Swayze** - She's Like the Wind (*Dirty Dancing*)

03 **Eric Carmen** - Hungry Eyes (*Dirty Dancing*)

04 **Survivor** - Eye of the Tiger (*Rocky IV*)

05 **Orchestral Manoeuvres in the Dark** - If You Leave (*Pretty in Pink*)

06 **The Psychedelic Furs** - Pretty in Pink (*Pretty In Pink*)

07 **Peter Gabriel** - In Your Eyes (*Say Anything*)

08 **Berlin** - Take My Breath Away (*Top Gun*)

09 **Irene Cara** - Flashdance . . . What a Feeling (*Flashdance*)

32

10 **Michael Sembello** - Maniac (*Flashdance*)

11 **Kenny Loggins** - Footloose (*Footloose*)

12 **Denise Williams** - Let's Hear It for the Boy (*Footloose*)

13 **John Cougar** - Hurts So Good (*Footloose*)

14 **Lick the Tins** - Can't Help Falling In Love (*Some Kind of Wonderful*)

15 **Jackson Browne** - Somebody's Baby (*Fast Times At Ridgemont High*)

16 **Simple Minds** - Don't You (Forget About Me) (*The Breakfast Club*)

17 **The Pilmsouls** - Million Miles Away (*Valley Girl*)

18 **Josie Cotton** - Johnny, Are You Queer? (*Valley Girl*)

19 **Modern English** - I Melt with You (*Valley Girl*)

20 **Sparks** - Angst in My Pants (*Valley Girl*)

21 **Plastic Bertrand** - Ça plane pour moi (*European Vacation*)

22 **Bobby McFerrin** - Don't Worry, Be Happy (*Cocktail*)

23 **The Beach Boys** - Kokomo (*Cocktail*)

24 **Corey Hart** - Hold On (*Beverly Hills Cop II*)

25 **Harold Faltermeyer** - Axel F. (*Beverly Hills Cop*)

26 **Ray Parker Jr.** - Ghostbusters (*Ghostbusters*)\*

27 **Echo & the Bunnymen** - People Are Strange (*The Lost Boys*)

28 **Gerard McMann** - Cry Little Sister (Theme from *The Lost Boys*) (*The Lost Boys*)

29 **Cyndi Lauper** - Goonies 'R' Good Enough (*The Goonies*)

30 **Limahl** - The NeverEnding Story (*The NeverEnding Story*)

31 **Harry Belafonte** - The Banana Boat Song (Day-O) (*Beetlejuice*)

---

\* Ray Parker Jr. got sued by Huey Lewis for the similarities between "I Want a New Drug" and "Ghostbusters."

## 90s DANCEABLE SONGS

This list really strays from what would be classically known as the best dance songs to come from the nineties, mostly because those songs are pretty horrendous and came before Pro Tools and Swedish hitmakers arrived toward the very end of the decade.

ESSENTIAL GENRES

01 **Jesus Jones** - Right Here, Right Now
02 **Counting Crows** - Mr. Jones
03 **Gin Blossoms** - Hey Jealousy
04 **EMF** - Unbelievable
05 **Melanie C.** - I Turn to You
06 **Elastica** - Connection
07 **Sublime** - What I Got
08 **Stone Temple Pilots** - Vasoline
09 **Marcy Playground** - Sex and Candy
10 **Sugar Ray** - Fly*
11 **Ugly Kid Joe** - Everything About You
12 **Deep Blue Something** - Breakfast at Tiffany's
13 **Blur** - Parklife
14 **Backstreet Boys** - Everybody (Backstreet's Back)
15 **Bush** - Machinehead
16 **Soul Asylum** - Somebody to Shove

17 **James** - Laid**

18 **Britney Spears** - (You Drive Me) Crazy

19 **Spin Doctors** - Little Miss Can't Be Wrong

20 **Republica** - Ready to Go

21 **The New Radicals** - You Get What You Give

22 **Nirvana** - Smells Like Teen Spirit

23 **White Zombie** - More Human Than Human

24 **Nine Inch Nails** - Head Like a Hole

25 **Hole** - Violet

26 **Beck** - Where It's At

---

\*    Sugar Ray's lead singer, Mark McGrath, is now a television host.

\*\*   "'Laid' was never our idea of a single—it was barely two minutes long, for Chrissakes. Someone in the record company spotted it. Here's to 'Laid,' the best B side we ever made." —Tim Booth, James (singer)

## 90s SOUNDTRACK SONGS

I'm totally a girl who was fifteen in the mid-nineties. *Romeo + Juliet* and *Trainspotting* were, like, the shit to me. I listened to those soundtracks like it was the last time I'd ever get to listen to music. And you know what? To this day, I want to call up the music supervisors who made those mixes and thank them endlessly for turning me onto great bands. There were songs from other soundtracks that blew my mind as well. Here they are:

01 **Roy Orbison** - Oh, Pretty Woman (*Pretty Woman*)
02 **Roxette** - It Must Have Been Love (*Pretty Woman*)
03 **The Cardigans** - Lovefool (*Romeo + Juliet*)
04 **The Wannadies** - You and Me Song (*Romeo + Juliet*)
05 **New Order** - Temptation (*Trainspotting*)
06 **Sleeper** - Atomic (*Trainspotting*)
07 **Underworld** - Born Slippy (*Trainspotting*)
08 **Nine Inch Nails** - The Perfect Drug (*Lost Highway*)
09 **Cowboy Junkies** - Sweet Jane (*Natural Born Killers*)
10 **Juliette Lewis** - Born Bad (*Natural Born Killers*)
11 **Nine Inch Nails** - Dead Souls (*The Crow*)

12 **Whitney Houston** - I Will Always Love You (*The Bodyguard*)

13 **Edwyn Collins** - A Girl Like You (*Empire Records*)

14 **Coyote Shivers** - Sugarhigh (*Empire Records*)

15 **Rick Derringer** - Rock and Roll, Hoochie Koo (*Dazed and Confused*)

16 **Love Spit Love** - How Soon Is Now? (*The Craft*)

17 **Aerosmith** - I Don't Want to Miss a Thing (*Armageddon*)

18 **Divinyls** - I Touch Myself (*Austin Powers*)

19 **Jefferson Airplane** - White Rabbit (*Fear and Loathing in Las Vegas*)

20 **Feeder** - High (*Can't Hardly Wait*)

21 **Seal** - Kiss from a Rose (*Batman Forever*)

22 **Hole** - Gold Dust Woman (*The Crow: City of Angels*)

23 **The Muffs** - Kids in America (*Clueless*)

24 **Jill Sobule** - Supermodel (*Clueless*)

25 **The Verve** - Bittersweet Symphony (*Cruel Intentions*)

26 **No Doubt** - New (*Go*)

27 **Sixpence None The Richer** - Kiss Me (*She's All That*)

28 **Queen** - Bohemian Rhapsody (*Wayne's World*)

## ALTERNATIVE COUNTRY

What makes alt country different from country is that it's self-aware and possibly ironic: An alt-country song is a country song that might be considered a parody. Now, that's totally debatable, since lots of alt-country artists seem to be focused on making songs that are amazing rather than wondering if the tunes are ironic enough. Or maybe the songs are just so good that you don't even notice how ironic they are.

01 **Dwight Yoakam** - Honky Tonk Man
02 **Junior Brown** - My Wife Thinks You're Dead
03 **Derailers** - Just One More Time
04 **Lucinda Williams** - Sweet Old World
05 **Victoria Williams** - Summer of Drugs
06 **Lyle Lovett** - She's No Lady
07 **Uncle Tupelo** - No Depression
08 **Gillian Welch** - Revelator
09 **Old 97's** - Nineteen
10 **Whiskeytown** - Nervous Breakdown
11 **Clem Snide** - Joan Jett of Arc
12 **Victoria Williams** - Crazy Mary
13 **Lyle Lovett** - Cute as a Bug

14 **Gillian Welch** - My Morphine

15 **Clem Snide** - Long Lost Twin

16 **My Morning Jacket** - One Big Holiday

17 **Lambchop** - Nothing Adventurous Please

18 **Fruit Bats** - Seaweed

19 **The Jayhawks** - Blue

20 **Billy Bragg and Wilco** - California Stars

21 **Palace** - Work Hard/Play Hard

22 **Kinky Friedman** - God Bless John Wayne
(People Who Read *People* Magazine)

23 **BR549** - Bettie Bettie

24 **Drive-by Truckers** - Outfit

25 **David Allan Coe** - You Never Even Called Me
by My Name

26 **The Sadies** - Loved on Look

27 **The Gourds** - I Like Drinking

28 **Waylon Jennings** - Luckenbach, Texas (Back
to the Basics of Love)

29 **Neko Case** - The Tigers Have Spoken

30 **Robert Earl Keen** - The Road Goes on Forever

31 **John Eddie** - Play Some Skynyrd

32 **The Damnations** - Bloodhound

33 **Southern Culture on the Skids** - Too Much
Pork for Just One Fork

34 **Jimmie Dale Gilmore** - Dallas

35 **Meat Puppets** - Lost

36 **Hayseed Dixie** - Let's Put the X in Sex

## AMBIENT

Chill out; relax; don't think. Just focus on the fact that you're now floating in space as little shapes fly across the sky and into the moon. If you're not feeling it, the ambient music will help bring you there.

01 **Popol Vuh** - *Aguirre*
02 **Aphex Twin** - Donkey Rhubarb
03 **David Bowie** - Subterraneans
04 **Brainticket** - Cosmic Wind
05 **Brian Eno** - 2/2
06 **White Noise** - The Black Mass: An Electric Storm in Hell
07 **Klaus Schulze** - Voices of Syn
08 **Can** - Unfinished
09 **Suicide** - Cheree
10 **Radiohead** - Treefingers
11 **Kraftwerk** - *Harmonika*
12 **Brian Eno** - A Clearing
13 **Tangerine Dream** - Circulation of Events
14 **Cul de Sac** - Death of the Sun
15 **Popol Vuh** - *In Den Gärten Pharaos*
16 **Neu!** - *Weissensee*

17 **Ash Ra Tempel** - *Traummaschine*

18 **Godspeed You Black Emperor** - Antennas to Heaven

19 **Can** - *Aumgn*

20 **Kraftwerk** - *Kometenmelodie*

21 **Cabaret Voltaire** - Cooled Out

22 **Mogwai** - Kids Will Be Skeletons

23 **Throbbing Gristle** - Beachy Head

24 **Sigur Rós** - Untitled 5

25 **Radiohead** - Like Spinning Plates

ESSENTIAL GENRES

## BLUES

> The Blues had a baby and they called it Rock 'n' Roll.

01 **Sonny Boy Williamson (II)** - Bring It On Home
02 **Lightnin' Hopkins** - Mojo Hand
03 **Willie Dixon** - Back Door Man
04 **John Lee Hooker** - Boom Boom
05 **Muddy Waters** - I Want You to Love Me
06 **Howlin' Wolf** - Smokestack Lightning
07 **Little Walter** - My Babe
08 **Elmore James** - Dust My Broom
09 **Etta James** - At Last
10 **Robert Johnson** - Cross Road Blues
11 **Walker** - Stormy Monday Blues
12 **Big Mama Thornton** - Hound Dog
13 **Buddy Guy** - Let Me Love You Baby
14 **Bo Diddley** - Who Do You Love?
15 **B.B. King** - The Thrill Is Gone
16 **Lead Belly** - In the Pines*
17 **Screamin' Jay Hawkins** - I Put a Spell on You**

---

\*    Covered by Nirvana for *Unplugged in New York*.

\*\*   Screamin' Jay Hawkins was an outrageous performer, given to emerging out of coffins onstage with a flaming skull named Henry in tow.

## BRAZILIAN MIX

Put on skimpy clothes and go somewhere heated, because now you have music to sweat to.

01 **Gal Costa** - *A Rita*
02 **Antonio Carlos Jobim** - *Aguas de Marco* (Waters of March)
03 **João Gilberto** - *Aquarela do Brasil*
04 **Caetano Veloso** - *Beleza Pura*
05 **Caetano Veloso** - *Chuvas de Verão*
06 **Rita Ribeiro** - *Cocada*
07 **Caetano Veloso** - *Coração Vagabundo*
08 **Sylvia Telles** - *Corcovado*
09 **Marisa Monte** - *Dança da Solidão*
10 **Marisa Monte** - *De Noite na Cama*
11 **Chico Da Silva** - *E Preciso Muito Amor*
12 **Agepê** - *Ela Não Gosta de Mim*
13 **João Gilberto** - *Falsa Baiana*
14 **Agepê** - *Feira de Mangaio*
15 **Celso Machado** - *Feliz, Felicidade*
16 **Didá Banda Feminina** - *Filhos do Tempo*
17 **Ciro Monteiro** - *Formosa*
18 **Sergio Mendes** - *Garôta de Ipanema* (The Girl From Ipanema)

ESSENTIAL GENRES

19 **Caetano Veloso** - *Lua de São Jorge*

20 **Ivette Sangalo** - *Monsieur Samba*

21 **Marisa Monte** - *Mustapha*

22 **Caetano Veloso** - *Na Baixa do Sapateiro*

23 **Alcione** - *Oleré Camará*

24 **Gal Costa** - *País Tropical*

25 **Sergio Mendes and Brasil '66** - *País Tropical*

26 **Zeca Pagodinho** - *SPC*

27 **Bebel Gilberto** - *Samba da Benção*

28 **Antonio Carlos Jobim** - *Samba de Una Nota So*

29 **Gal Costa** - *Samba do Grande Amor*

30 **Suba** - *Samba do Gringo Paulista*

31 **Elis Regina** - *Triste*

## BRIT POP

If you were British and in a band in the mid-
nineties, life was probably pretty sweet.
Somehow, in the span of a few years, one little
island managed to produce more good songs than
anyone could have ever imagined.

01 **Oasis** - Wonderwall
02 **Blur** - Girls & Boys
03 **Elastica** - Connection
04 **Oasis** - Live Forever
05 **Suede** - Trash
06 **Pulp** - Common People
07 **Supergrass** - Alright
08 **Pulp** - Disco 2000
09 **Travis** - All I Want to Do Is Rock
10 **The Stone Roses** - I Wanna Be Adored
11 **Blur** - Parklife
12 **Blur** - Song 2
13 **The La's** - There She Goes
14 **James** - Laid
15 **Longpigs** - On and On
16 **Republica** - Ready to Go
17 **Spiritualized** - Come Together

18 **The Verve** - Bittersweet Symphony

19 **Placebo** - Nancy Boy

20 **Primal Scream** - Movin' on Up

21 **Ash** - Kung Fu

22 **Gene** - Haunted by You

23 **Mansun** - Wide Open Space

24 **Manic Street Preachers** - A Design for Life

25 **Menswear** - Daydreamer

26 **The Charlatans UK** - North Country Boy

27 **Lush** - Ladykillers

## CLASSIC ROCK

Apart from the common thread of being from the same era, there's a reason the term "classic" refers to this music. These songs are undeniably timeless, and no matter what else the artists on this list have released over the years, they are absolved of all questionable musical offenses.

ESSENTIAL GENRES

01 **The Rolling Stones** - Brown Sugar
02 **The Beatles** - Day in the Life
03 **Led Zeppelin** - Stairway to Heaven
04 **Bob Dylan** - Like a Rolling Stone
05 **Jimi Hendrix** - Purple Haze
06 **The Who** - Baba O'Riley
07 **Rod Stewart** - Maggie May
08 **Janis Joplin** - Piece of My Heart
09 **Pink Floyd** - Money
10 **Aerosmith** - Walk this Way
11 **AC/DC** - Highway to Hell
12 **Fleetwood Mac** - Dreams
13 **The Eagles** - Hotel California
14 **KISS** - Rock and Roll All Nite
15 **The Greatful Dead** - Truckin'
16 **Black Sabbath** - Paranoid

17 **The Doors** - Light My Fire

18 **Neil Young** - Heart of Gold

19 **Lynyrd Skynyrd** - Free Bird

20 **ZZ Top** - Tush

21 **The Allman Brothers Band** - Ramblin' Man

22 **Deep Purple** - Smoke on the Water

23 **Elton John** - Rocket Man (I Think It's Going to Be a Long Long Time)

24 **David Bowie** - Changes

25 **Creedence Clearwater Revival** - Proud Mary

26 **Santana** - Black Magic Woman/Gypsy Queen

27 **Bad Company** - Feel Like Makin' Love

28 **Yes** - I've Seen All Good People

29 **Alice Cooper** - School's Out

30 **Eric Clapton** - Layla

31 **Van Halen** - You Really Got Me

## CLASSICAL

Everyone should have a classical music collection of some sort. Not because classical music is amazing, which it totally is, but also because it makes you look smart and diverse. Take it from me...when the workday becomes stressful and you really don't think you can take anymore of it, throw this mix on, and watch as life becomes a whole lot easier. It's also good for babies!

### SYMPHONIC

01 **Beethoven** - Symphony no. 3 in E-flat Major ("Eroica"), op. 55

02 **Beethoven** - Symphony no. 5 in C Minor ("Fate"), op.67

03 **Beethoven** - Symphony no. 9 in D Minor ("Choral"), op. 125

04 **Mozart** - Symphony no. 40 in G Minor, K. 550

05 **Schubert** - Symphony no. 9 in C Major ("The Great"), D. 944

06 **Brahms** - Symphony no. 4 in E Minor, op. 98

07 **Mahler** - Symphony no. 5 in C-sharp Minor

08 **Shostakovich** - Symphony no. 5 in D Minor, op. 47

09 **Stravinsky** - *The Rite of Spring*

ESSENTIAL GENRES

10 **Bartók** - Concerto for Orchestra

11 **Debussy** - *Prelude to the Afternoon of a Faun*

12 **Copland** - *Appalachian Spring*

## CHAMBER MUSIC

13 **Beethoven** - String Quartets nos. 1-3, op. 59

14 **Schubert** - String Quartet no. 14
in D Minor ("Death and the Maiden"), D. 810

15 **Brahms** - Piano Quintet in F Minor, op. 34a

16 **Bartók** - String Quartets nos. 1-6

## PIANO MUSIC

17 **Bach** - *Goldberg Variations*

18 **Beethoven** - Piano Sonata no. 21
in C Major ("Waldstein"), op. 53

19 **Beethoven** - Piano Sonata, no. 14
in C-sharp Minor ("Moonlight"), op. 27/2

20 **Beethoven** - Piano Sonata no. 29
in B-flat Major ("Hammerklavier"), op. 106

21 **Mozart** - Piano Concertos no. 23
in A Major, K. 488, and no. 20 D Minor, K. 466

22 **Chopin** - Complete Preludes

23 **Debussy** - Complete Preludes

24 **Ravel** - *Gaspard de la nuit*

## COUNTRY

Your wife left you for your brother and your dog ran away with the shoe. Country music tells it like it is. No guessing, no fooling around, just straight-up storytelling about how bad life is, how bad it can be, and how bad it'll get. America LOVES country music, but a lot of people would say, "I like all music except for country." Here are country songs that will make you change your tune.

01 **George Jones** - The Race Is On
02 **Willie Nelson** - Blue Eyes Crying in the Rain
03 **Merle Haggard** - Okie From Muskogee
04 **Kris Kristofferson** - Sunday Morning Coming Down
05 **Johnny Cash** - I Walk the Line
06 **Hank Williams** - Lovesick Blues
07 **Jimmie Rodgers** - T for Texas
08 **Charlie Rich** - Most Beautiful Girl
09 **Chet Atkins** - Mr. Sandman
10 **Bob Wills & His Texas Playboys** - New San Antonio Rose
11 **Dolly Parton** - Jolene

12 **Patsy Cline** - Crazy

13 **Loretta Lynn** - Coal Miner's Daughter

14 **Tammy Wynette** - Stand by Your Man

15 **Wanda Jackson** - Riot in Cell Block #9

16 **Ray Price** - Crazy Arms

17 **Roy Acuff** - The Great Speckled Bird

18 **The Carter Family** - Wabash Cannonball

19 **Bill Monroe** - Kentucky Waltz

20 **Dwight Yoakam** - Guitars, Cadillacs

21 **Gram Parsons** - Sin City

## DISCO

Everyone says that this genre is dead, but I know that it's just taking a disco nap.

01 **Kool & the Gang** - Celebration
02 **Bee Gees** - Stayin' Alive
03 **Sylvia Striplin** - Give Me Your Love
04 **Gwen Guthrie** - Ain't Nothin' Goin' On But The Rent
05 **Central Line** - Walking Into Sunshine
06 **Loose Joints** - Is It All Over My Face?
07 **Dinosaur L** - Go Bang
08 **Jimmy "Bo" Horne** - Spank
09 **Kool & the Gang** - Get Down on It
10 **The O'Jays** - Love Train
11 **The Emotions** - Best of My Love
12 **Tavares** - More Than a Woman
13 **Hot Chocolate** - You Sexy Thing
14 **Chic** - Good Times
15 **Sister Sledge** - He's the Greatest Dancer
16 **Rose Royce** - Car Wash
17 **Denroy Morgan** - I'll Do Anything for You
18 **Carl Carlton** - Everlasting Love
19 **Donna Summer** - Hot Stuff

20 **Bee Gees** - Jive Talkin'

21 **Yvonne Elliman** - If I Can't Have You

22 **Earth, Wind & Fire** - September

23 **Roy Ayers** - Running Away

24 **KC and the Sunshine Band** - (Shake, Shake, Shake) Shake Your Booty

25 **Lipps Inc.** - Funkytown

26 **Diana Ross** - Upside Down

27 **Weather Girls** - It's Raining Men

28 **Thelma Houston** - Don't Leave Me This Way

29 **Donna Summer** - I Feel Love

**ESSENTIAL GENRES**

## ELECTRONIC

In 1997, music magazines all around the world declared rock dead, suggesting that electronic music would be the next big thing. They were sort of wrong (depending on who you ask), but regardless, you can't deny the music that came from, and was a result of, that era.

**ESSENTIAL GENRES**

01 **Les Rythmes Digitales** - (Hey You) What's That Sound?

02 **The Chemical Brothers** - Block Rockin' Beats

03 **Basement Jaxx** - Where's Your Head At

04 **Fatboy Slim** - Right Here, Right Now

05 **The Prodigy** - Breathe

06 **The Chemical Brothers** - Setting Sun*

07 **Lo Fidelity Allstars** - Battle Flag

08 **Underworld** - Born Slippy

09 **The Chemical Brothers** - Out of Control**

10 **Daft Punk** - Around the World

11 **Fatboy Slim** - The Rockafeller Skank

12 **Basement Jaxx** - Romeo

13 **Daft Punk** - One More Time

14 **The Crystal Method** - Busy Child

15 **Death in Vegas** - Dirt

16 **Stardust** - Music Sounds Better with You

17 **Basement Jaxx** - Rendez-Vu

18 **Fatboy Slim** - Praise You

\*     Features Noel Gallagher from Oasis

\*\*    Features Bernard Sumner from New Order

ESSENTIAL GENRES

## EMO

### DO THE EMO-LUTION

"When I discovered this music, I wasn't a teen-ager. I wasn't a rebel. I wasn't crashing school dances. I wasn't working a dead-end job. I wasn't breaking up with my boyfriend. I wasn't shopping at Hot Topic. I wasn't sneaking into R-rated movies. I wasn't looking to be saved, and yet this music changed my life. It might not alter yours, but I guarantee it'll offer an amazing sound-track." —Leslie Simon, *Alternative Press* (editor)

01 **Sunny Day Real Estate** - In Circles
02 **Weezer** - Say It Ain't So
03 **Jawbreaker** - Save Your Generation
04 **The Get Up Kids** - Don't Hate Me
05 **Lifetime** - Turnpike Gates
06 **Braid** - Never Will Come for Us
07 **Jimmy Eat World** - Lucky Denver Mint
08 **The Promise Ring** - Emergency! Emergency!
09 **The Anniversary** - The Heart Is a Lonely Hunter
10 **Bright Eyes** - Haligh, Haligh, a Lie, Haligh
11 **Rainer Maria** - Artificial Light
12 **Reggie and the Full Effect** - Thanx for Stayin'

13 **Alkaline Trio** - Take Lots with Alcohol

14 **Brand New** - Mix Tape

15 **Dashboard Confessional** - The Best Deceptions

16 **Saves the Day** - Firefly

17 **Thursday** - Understanding in a Car Crash

18 **Piebald** - American Hearts

19 **Taking Back Sunday** - Timberwolves at New Jersey

20 **Fall Out Boy** - Chicago Is So Two Years Ago

21 **Motion City Soundtrack** - My Favorite Accident

## FOLK

Morrissey once sang, "I thought that if you had an acoustic guitar then it meant that you were a protest singer," which would describe much of the early days of folk music. But the genre has grown to describe narrative songs sung by people on acoustic guitars.

01 **Bob Dylan** - The Times They Are A-Changin'
02 **Neil Young** - Revolution Blues
03 **Joni Mitchell** - A Case of You
04 **Tom Waits** - (Looking For) The Heart of Saturday Night
05 **Bruce Springsteen** - Atlantic City
06 **Leonard Cohen** - Suzanne
07 **Van Morrison** - Astral Weeks
08 **Crosby, Stills, Nash & Young** - Ohio
09 **Nick Drake** - Northern Sky
10 **Elvis Costello** - Alison
11 **John Lennon** - Oh Yoko!
12 **Dave Van Ronk** - Gambler's Blues
13 **Pete Seeger** - We Shall Overcome
14 **Simon & Garfunkel** - Scarborough Fair/Canticle

15 **Ramblin' Jack Elliot** - More Pretty Girls

16 **Woody Guthrie** - This Land Is Your Land

17 **Elliott Smith** - Miss Misery

18 **Joan Baez** - Diamonds & Rust

19 **The Mamas & the Papas** - Dream a Little Dream of Me

20 **James Taylor** - Don't Let Me Be Lonely Tonight

21 **Donovan** - Mellow Yellow

22 **Jeff Buckley** - Last Goodbye

23 **Lou Reed** - Perfect Day

24 **The Byrds** - Turn! Turn! Turn!

## FUNK

Welcome to Funky Town. Population: You. If you ever plan on playing bass in a band, this list is a requirement. Funk is all about getting down, partying, and shakin' your rumpity bump.

01 **Funkadelic** - (Not Just) Knee Deep
02 **George Clinton** - Atomic Dog
03 **The Commodores** - Brick House
04 **The Meters** - Cissy Strut
05 **James Brown** - Get Up (I Feel Like Being A) Sex Machine
06 **Brick** - Dazz
07 **Sly & the Family Stone** - Family Affair
08 **Parliament** - Give Up the Funk (Tear the Roof off the Sucker)
09 **Kool & the Gang** - Jungle Boogie
10 **Rick James** - Super Freak
11 **Curtis Mayfeild** - Superfly
12 **Stevie Wonder** - Superstition
13 **Isaac Hayes** - Theme from *Shaft*
14 **Prince** - Dirty Mind
15 **Chic** - Good Times
16 **Patti LaBelle** - Lady Marmalade

17 **Neville Brothers** - Fire On The Bayou

18 **Average White Band** - Pick Up The Pieces

19 **Wild Cherry** - Play That Funky Music

20 **Bootsy Collins** - The Pinocchio Theory

21 **War** - Why Can't We Be Friends?

22 **Cameo** - Word Up!

23 **Gap Band** - You Dropped a Bomb on Me

24 **Hot Chocolate** - You Sexy Thing

## GLAM ROCK

While glam rock is sort of a forgotten genre, it has influenced the widest array of bands imaginable—everyone from Mötley Crüe to Radiohead. Its sound lives on in bands such as Muse, Franz Ferdinand, Placebo, and Interpol. For more about glam rock, check out the film *Velvet Goldmine*.

**ESSENTIAL GENRES**

01 **T. Rex** - Cosmic Dancer
02 **Roxy Music** - More Than This
03 **Roxy Music** - Ladytron
04 **David Bowie** - All The Young Dudes
05 **T. Rex** - 20th Century Boy
06 **New York Dolls** - Personality Crisis
07 **David Bowie** - Suffragette City
08 **Brian Eno** - Baby's on Fire
09 **Roxy Music** - 2HB
10 **Gary Glitter** - Do You Wanna Touch Me? (Oh Yeah!)
11 **T. Rex** - Jeepster
12 **Jobriath** - I'm a Man*
13 **Queen** - Killer Queen
14 **Lou Reed** - Perfect Day
15 **Lou Reed** - Satellite of Love

16 **Gary Glitter** - Rock & Roll, Pt. 2**
17 **Sweet** - Little Willy
18 **Slade** - Cum on Feel the Noize

---

\*   The Smiths' lead singer, Morrissey, was a huge fan of the tragic figure Jobriath, who was the first openly gay rock star. After a failed career, Jobriath died of an AIDS-related illness in 1983.

\*\*  It's quite possible that this song has been used at every single sporting event of the past thirty years.

---

## GOTH

In New York City there's a bimonthly party called "Visions of the Impending Apocalypse." It's a fashionable goth party, and the DJs really know their stuff. The group that brought NYC the best goth party brings you the definitive goth mix.

01 **No More** - Suicide Commando
02 **DAF** - *Der Mussolini*
03 **Pankow** - Germany Is Burning
04 **Clan of Xymox** - Muscoviet Musquito
05 **Acid Horse** - No Name, No Slogan
06 **Inca Babies** - The Interior
07 **Trisomie 21** - Sunken Lives
08 **Malaria** - Your Turn to Run
09 **Big Black** - Precious Thing
10 **Bone Orchard** - Lynched
11 **Modern Eon** - Mechanic
12 **Click Click** - Yakutska
13 **The Wake** - Judas
14 **Asylum Party** - Play Alone
15 **Sisters of Mercy** - Lucretia My Reflection
16 **Death Cult** - God's Zoo (These Times)
17 **And One** - *Deutschmachine*

18 **Red Lorry Yellow Lorry** - Generation
19 **Front Line Assembly** - Provision
20 **Camouflage** - The Great Commandment
21 **Skinny Puppy** - Tin Omen
22 **Killing Joke** - Love Like Blood
23 **The Misfits** - Last Caress
24 **KMFDM** - Megalomaniac
25 **Siouxsie and the Banshees** - Monitor

## GRUNGE

The term "Grunge" was pretty much invented as an easy way to describe punk rock played by people with long, unwashed hair and an affinity for flannel. This is not to say that I wasn't totally obsessed with it when I was growing up. And as far as the music industry is concerned, Nirvana is the greatest band ever.

ESSENTIAL GENRES

01 **Nirvana** - Lithium
02 **Hole** - Miss World
03 **Pearl Jam** - Jeremy*
04 **Soul Asylum** - Runaway Train
05 **Soundgarden** - Black Hole Sun
06 **Pearl Jam** - Even Flow
07 **Temple of the Dog** - Hunger Strike**
08 **Screaming Trees** - Nearly Lost You
09 **Stone Temple Pilots** - Plush
10 **Nirvana** - Come as You Are
11 **L7** - Pretend We're Dead
12 **Mudhoney** - Touch Me I'm Sick
13 **Stone Temple Pilots** - Big Empty
14 **Nirvana** - Smells Like Teen Spirit
15 **Candlebox** - Far Behind

16 **Bush** - Everything Zen

17 **Alice in Chains**- Rooster

18 **Babes in Toyland** - Bruise Violet

19 **Nirvana** - Heart Shaped Box

20 **Everclear** - Santa Monica

21 **Bush** - Glycerine

---

\* Pearl Jam's lead singer, Eddie Vedder, appeared in the zeitgeist film *Singles*, which was directed by Cameron Crowe.

\*\* Two popular grunge bands, Soundgarden and Pearl Jam, formed Temple of the Dog.

## HARDCORE

Aggressive, noisy guitars. Vocals that sound like they were processed through a blender. And yet through all that chaos, hardcore music manages to be not only rhythmic but also harmonic.

01 **1.6 Band** - Back in Church
02 **Killing Time** - Backtrack
03 **Burn** - . . . Shall Be Judged
04 **The Faith** - Subject to Change
05 **Verbal Assault** - Trial
06 **Underdog** - True Blue
07 **Underdog** - Frontside Grind
08 **The Meatmen** - Meatmen Stomp
09 **Bad Brains** - Soul Craft
10 **Bl'ast!** - Time to Think/Surf and Destroy
11 **Chain of Strength** - True Till Death
12 **The Circle Jerks** - Parade of the Horribles
13 **The Circle Jerks** - In Your Eyes
14 **CIV** - Set Your Goals
15 **Descendents** - Clean Sheets
16 **D.Y.S.** - Which Side Am I
17 **D.Y.S.** - City to City
18 **Faction** - Tongue Like a Battering Ram

19 **Gorilla Biscuits** - New Direction
20 **Gorilla Biscuits** - Big Mouth
21 **Gorilla Biscuits** - Hold Your Ground
22 **JFA** - Beach Blanket Bongout
23 **Murphy's Law** - Murphy's Law
24 **Murphy's Law** - California Pipeline
25 **Negative Approach** - Lost Cause
26 **Scream** - Came Without Warning
27 **Soul Side** - Punch the Geek
28 **Suicidal Tendencies** - Possessed to Skate
29 **The Abused** - Loud And Clear
30 **Half Off** - The Truth
31 **T.S.O.L.** - Superficial Love
32 **T.S.O.L.** - Code Blue
33 **Krakdown** - Ignorance
34 **Void** - Who Are You?

## HIP-HOP

No matter what kind of music you like, you can't deny the absolutely addictive qualities of some hip-hop songs. There's a good reason for that: Hip-hop is awesome. Here are some songs you need in your collection.

01 **The Notorious B.I.G.** - Big Poppa
02 **2Pac** - California Love
03 **Public Enemy** - Don't Believe the Hype
04 **Beastie Boys** - Brass Monkey
05 **Run-D.M.C.** - It's Like That
06 **De La Soul** - Me, Myself and I
07 **A Tribe Called Quest** - Scenario
08 **Dr. Dre** - Nuthin' but a "G" Thang
09 **B.G.** - Bling Bling
10 **Public Enemy** - 911 Is a Joke
11 **Jay-Z** - Hard Knock Life (Ghetto Anthem)
12 **Dr. Dre** - Let Me Ride
13 **2Pac** - Me Against the World
14 **Outkast** - B.O.B.
15 **DMX** - Party Up (Up In Here)
16 **Strafe** - Set It Off
17 **N.W.A.** - Straight Outta Compton

18 **Jay-Z** - Big Pimpin'
19 **Eminem** - Lose Yourself
20 **Snoop Doggy Dogg** - Who Am I? (What's My Name)?
21 **Rob Base** - It Takes Two
22 **Missy Elliott** - Work It
23 **Jay-Z** - 99 Problems
24 **Ol' Dirty Bastard** - Got Your Money
25 **Mystikal** - Shake Ya Ass
26 **Wu-Tang Clan** - Protect Ya Neck
27 **Run-D.M.C.** - Walk This Way
28 **Lil' Kim** - Magic Stick

## HIP-HOP OLD SCHOOL

Hip-hop is one of the newer types of music, and much like its predecessor rock 'n' roll, nobody thought it would ever last. Everyone was certain it was just a fad, but unlike many things in the '80s, hip-hop's influence grew exponentially. Here's where it started.

01 **Grandmaster Flash and the Furious Five** - The Adventures of Grandmaster Flash on the Wheels of Steel
02 **Fat Boys** - Fat Boys
03 **The World Class Wreckin' Cru** - Surgery
04 **Beastie Boys** - Rhymin' and Stealin'
05 **Spoonie Gee** - Love Rap
06 **ESG** - UFO
07 **Grandmaster Flash and the Furious Five** - The Message
08 **Kurtis Blow** - The Breaks
09 **Dana Dane** - Nightmares
10 **Kool Moe Dee** - I Go to Work
11 **Whodini** - Freaks Come out at Night
12 **Grandmixer D.ST** - Crazy Cuts
13 **Kurtis Blow** - Basketball

14 **L'Trimm** - Cars with the Boom
15 **Afrika Bambaataa** - Looking for the Perfect
   Beat
16 **Spoonie Gee** - Monster Jam
17 **Davy DMX** - One for the Treble
18 **The Sugarhill Gang** - Rapper's Delight
19 **Grandmaster Flash and the Furious Five** -
   White Lines (Don't Don't Do It)
20 **Newcleus** - Jam on Revenge (The Wikki-
   Wikki Song)

## HIP-HOP/R & B CHEESY DANCE PARTY

The title of this list is pretty self-explanatory: These are cheesy hip-hop/R & B songs. The sad thing is that I know all the lyrics to all of them, and I bet you do too. You'd be surprised by how much of a hit these are at any party.

01 **Quad City DJ's** - C'mon N' Ride It (The Train)
02 **Marky Mark and the Funky Bunch** - Good Vibrations
03 **Wreckx-N-Effect** - Rump Shaker
04 **69 Boyz** - Tootsee Roll
05 **MC Hammer** - U Can't Touch This
06 **Tag Team** - Whoomp! (There It Is)
07 **2 Live Crew** - Me So Horny
08 **K7** - Come Baby Come
09 **Naughty By Nature** - O.P.P.
10 **Sir Mix-a-Lot** - Baby Got Back
11 **Tone Loc** - Wild Thing
12 **Vanilla Ice** - Ice Ice Baby
13 **Rico Suave** - Gerardo
14 **Color Me Badd** - I Wanna Sex You Up
15 **En Vogue** - My Lovin' (You're Never Gonna Get It)
16 **Keith Sweat** - Make You Sweat

ESSENTIAL GENRES

17 **Blackstreet** - No Diggity

18 **C+C Music Factory** - Gonna Make You Sweat
   (Everybody Dance Now)

19 **Rick Astley** - Never Gonna Give You Up

20 **Snap** - The Power

21 **Stereo MC's** - Connected

22 **Technotronic** - Pump Up the Jam

23 **Milli Vanilli** - Girl You Know It's True

24 **Debbie Gibson** - Only In My Dreams

25 **Spice Girls** - Wannabe

26 **Deee-Lite** - Groove Is in the Heart

27 **Ace of Base** - The Sign

## HOUSE

Partying in Ibiza brought to your MP3 player by international superstar DJ Junior Sanchez.

ESSENTIAL GENRES

01 **Lil' Louis** - French Kiss
02 **A Guy Called Gerald** - Voodoo Ray
03 **Jungle Brothers** - I'll House You
04 **Saint Etienne** - Only Love Can Break Your Heart
05 **Aphrohead** - In Thee Dark We Live (Dave Clarke Mix)
06 **Tyree** - Acid Crash (bootleg, never officially released)
07 **Fingers Inc.** - Can You Feel It
08 **Bobby Konders** - The Poem
09 **Björk** - Violently Happy (Masters at Work Remix)
10 **Pal Joey** - Earth People Dance Groove
11 **Nightcrawlers** - Push the Feeling On (MK Mix)
12 **Jaydee** - Plastic Dreams
13 **Coldcut** (featuring Lisa Stansfield) - People Hold On
14 **Sterling Void** - It's All Right
15 **Stardust** - Music Sounds Better with You

16 **Renegade Soundwave** - The Phantom
17 **Ralphi Rosario** (featuring Xavier Gold) -
   You Used to Hold Me
18 **Daft Punk** - Around the World
19 **CLS** - Can You Feel It
20 **Liberty City** - Some Lovin'
21 **Those Guys** - Tonite
22 **Joey Beltram** - Energy Flash
23 **Urban Soul** - Alright
24 **Adonis** - No Way Back
25 **Sandee** - Notice Me

## INDIE DANCE PARTY

For the ladies who want to be with Seth Cohen and the boys who want to be him.

01 **The Von Bondies** - C'mon C'mon
02 **Joy Division** - Love Will Tear Us Apart
03 **Le Tigre** - Deceptacon
04 **Yeah Yeah Yeahs** - Date with the Night
05 **James** - Laid
06 **Sparks** - Angst in My Pants
07 **Franz Ferdinand** - Take Me Out
08 **Bloc Party** - Banquet
09 **The Killers** - Somebody Told Me
10 **The Postal Service** - Such Great Heights
11 **Arcade Fire** - Rebellion (Lies)
12 **Iggy Pop** - Lust for Life
13 **The Bravery** - An Honest Mistake
14 **Blondie** - Atomic
15 **TV on the Radio** - Staring at the Sun
16 **Depeche Mode** - Personal Jesus
17 **INXS** - Need You Tonight
18 **Interpol** - Slow Hands
19 **The Cure** - Lovesong
20 **The Go! Team** - Huddle Formation

ESSENTIAL GENRES

21 **Elastica** - Connection
22 **Razorlight** - Rip It Up
23 **Modest Mouse** - Float On
24 **The Strokes** - Last Nite
25 **Pulp** - Common People
26 **New Order** - Crystal
27 **Pixies** - Debaser
28 **The Rapture** - House of Jealous Lovers
29 **Kasabian** - Club Foot
30 **Johnny Boy** - You Are the Generation That Bought More Shoes and You Get What You Deserve

## INDUSTRIAL

If dance music mixed with a metal edge—or metal with a dance groove—sounds dope to you, then you're checking out the right list.

01 **Skinny Puppy** - Tin Omen
02 **Front 242** - Headhunter
03 **KMFDM** - Juke-Joint Jezebel
04 **Nitzer Ebb** - Warsaw Ghetto
05 **Ministry** - Stigmata
06 **Front Line Assembly** - Resist
07 **:wumpscut:** - Soylent Green
08 **Pigface** - Fuck It Up
09 **Nine Inch Nails** - Head Like A Hole
10 **And One** - *Deutschmaschine*
11 **Throbbing Gristle** - Hamburger Lady
12 **My Life With the Thrill Kill Kult** - Sex on Wheelz
13 **Tricky** - Pre-Millennium Tension
14 **Severed Heads** - Spastic Crunch
15 **Coil** - Love's Secret Domain
16 **Suicide** - Ghost Rider
17 **Cabaret Voltaire** - Nag Nag Nag
18 **Revolting Cocks** - Do Ya Think I'm Sexy

ESSENTIAL GENRES

19 **Haujobb** - Rising Sun

20 **Meat Beat Manifesto** - God O.D.

21 **Psychic TV** - United '94

22 **Cubanate** - An Airport Bar

23 **Signal Aout 42** - Pleasure and Crime

24 **Einstürzende Neubauten** - Headcleaner

25 **Rammstein** - *Du Hast*

## JAZZ

There are about ninety-three million good jazz songs out there, but here are the basics. Should you ever work at a coffee shop, this is the mix that should be playing all day long.

01 **Miles Davis** - So What
02 **Louis Armstrong** - West End Blues
03 **Duke Ellington** - Black and Tan Fantasy
04 **Billie Holiday** - Strange Fruit
05 **John Coltrane** - Giant Steps
06 **Miles Davis** - Summertime
07 **Artie Shaw** - In the Mood
08 **Coleman Hawkins** - Body and Soul
09 **Bud Powell** - A Night in Tunisia
10 **Bill Evans** - My Man's Gone Now
11 **Dave Brubeck** - Take Five
12 **Art Blakey** - Caravan
13 **Sarah Vaughan** - My Funny Valentine
14 **Ella Fitzgerald** - How High the Moon
15 **Charlie Parker** - Koko
16 **Charles Mingus** - Pithecanthropus Erectus
17 **Louis Armstrong** - (What Did I Do to Be So) Black and Blue

18 **Artie Shaw** - My Blue Heaven

19 **Charles Mingus** - E's Flat, Ah's Flat Too

20 **Thelonious Monk** - 'Round Midnight

21 **Miles Davis** - Stella by Starlight

22 **Duke Ellington** - It Don't Mean a Thing (If It Ain't Got That Swing)

23 **Miles Davis** - Freddie Freeloader

24 **Frank Sinatra** - My Way

25 **Jelly Roll Morton** - King Porter Stomp

26 **Ella Fitzgerald** - They Can't Take That Away From Me

## MASH-UPS

ESSENTIAL GENRES

"Mash-up" and "bootleg" are terms used to describe the combination of two totally different yet recognizable songs that are typically unauthorized. The titles usually have "vs." in the name to reference the two songs used to create one track. The mash-up craze started in 2001 when a DJ known as Freelance Hellraiser mashed together Christina Aguilera's "Genie in a Bottle" and the Strokes' "Hard to Explain" in a track called "A Stroke of Genius." And in 2004, DJ/producer Danger Mouse combined Jay-Z's *The Black Album* with the Beatles' *The White Album* to produce the underground sensation *The Grey Album*.

01 **The Freelance Hellraiser** - A Stroke of Genius (Christina Aguilera's "Genie in a Bottle" vs. The Strokes' "Hard to Explain")

02 **Soulwax** - Smells Like Booty (Nirvana's "Smells Like Teen Spirit" vs. Destiny's Child's "Bootylicious")

03 **Danger Mouse** - 99 Problems (Jay-Z's "99 Problems" vs. The Beatles' "Helter Skelter")

04 **Party Ben** - Somebody Rock Me (The Killers' "Somebody Told Me" vs. The Clash's "Rock the Casbah")

05 **Erol Alkan** - Can't Get Blue Monday Out of My Head (Kylie Minogue's "Can't Get You Out of My Head" vs. New Order's "Blue Monday")*

06 **A Plus D** - Decepta-Freak-On (Missy Elliott's "Get Ur Freak On" vs. Le Tigre's "Deceptacon")

07 **Go Home Productions** - Ray of Gob (Madonna's "Ray of Light" vs. Sex Pistols' "Pretty Vacant" and "God Save the Queen")

08 **Go Home Productions** - Rapture Riders (The Doors' "Riders on the Storm" vs. Blondie's "Rapture")

09 **Ultra 396**- Intergalactic Friends (Beastie Boys' "Intergalactic" vs. The Dandy Warhols' "We Used to Be Friends")

10 **Dsico** - Love Will Freak Us (Missy Elliott's "Get Ur Freak On" vs. Joy Division's "Love Will Tear Us Apart")

11 **The Freelance Hellraiser** - Just Can't Get Enough Pills (Depeche Mode's "Just Can't Get Enough" vs. D12's "Purple Pills")

---

\* Kylie Minogue performed this version at the Brit Awards in 2002. This was the first known live performance of a mash-up by a major artist.

The best mash-up Web site on the Internet is http://boomselection.info/.

## METAL

Many people are quite sure that metal is the devil's music, but the only real damage it causes is the headache induced by all the head banging.

01 **Judas Priest** - Breaking the Law
02 **Motörhead** - Ace of Spades
03 **Black Sabbath** - Luke's Wall/War Pigs
04 **Dio** - Last in Line
05 **Iron Maiden** - The Number of the Beast
06 **Metallica** - Creeping Death
07 **Anthrax** - Caught in a Mosh
08 **Slayer** - Angel of Death
09 **Exodus** - Bonded by Blood
10 **Scorpions** - Rock You Like a Hurricane
11 **Megadeth** - Peace Sells
12 **Saxon** - Denim and Leather
13 **Mercyful Fate** - Evil
14 **Mayhem** - Deathcrush
15 **Pantera** - Walk
16 **Sepultura** - Slave New World
17 **Voivod** - Killing Technology
18 **Accept** - Balls to the Wall
19 **Morbid Angel** - Chapel of Ghouls

## MOTOWN

One record label created more superstars and amazing songs than any other out there, and that label is Motown. It's where Michael Jackson, Diana Ross, and Stevie Wonder all got their start, and its catalog is insane. Here are some of the best Motown tunes.

01 **Martha and the Vandellas** - (Love Is Like a) Heat Wave
02 **The Four Tops** - I Can't Help Myself (Sugar Pie, Honey Bunch)
03 **Marvin Gaye** - I Heard It Through the Grapevine
04 **The Temptations** - My Girl
05 **The Marvelettes** - Please Mr. Postman
06 **Stevie Wonder** - Signed, Sealed, Delivered, I'm Yours
07 **The Supremes** - Stop! In the Name of Love
08 **Smokey Robinson** - Tears of a Clown*
09 **The Supremes** - You Can't Hurry Love
10 **The Jackson 5** - ABC
11 **Marvin Gaye** - Ain't No Mountain High Enough
12 **The Temptations** - Ain't Too Proud to Beg
13 **The Supremes** - You Keep Me Hangin' On

14 **The Supremes** - (You Make Me Feel Like) A
Natural Woman
15 **The Supremes** - Baby Love
16 **The Temptations** - The Way You Do the
Things You Do
17 **Martha and the Vandellas** - Dancing in the
Street
18 **The Four Tops** - Reach Out (I'll Be There)
19 **Shorty Long** - Devil With a Blue Dress On
20 **The Temptations** - Papa Was a Rolling Stone
21 **Edwin Starr** - War
22 **Jackie Wilson** - (Your Love Keeps Lifting Me)
Higher and Higher
23 **Stevie Wonder** - Isn't She Lovely

ESSENTIAL GENRES

---

\*    This song was covered by the ska band the English Beat.

---

## NEW WAVE

For music that was once considered disposable, it's quite remarkable how well new wave has stood the test of time and constantly makes a comeback (or never goes away, depending on how you look at it). Almost any song from this list can be played anywhere, and everyone will recognize it.

01 **Bow Wow Wow** - I Want Candy
02 **Adam and the Ants** - Stand and Deliver
03 **A Flock Of Seagulls** -I Ran (So Far Away)
04 **The Cure** - Lovesong
05 **The Smiths** - How Soon is Now?
06 **Culture Club** - Karma Chameleon
07 **Bananarama** - Cruel Summer
08 **Go-Go's** - Our Lips Are Sealed
09 **Kajagoogoo** - Too Shy
10 **Talking Heads** - Road to Nowhere
11 **Gang of Four** - I Like a Man In Uniform
12 **Duran Duran** - Girls on Film
13 **Blondie** - Atomic
14 **Spandau Ballet** - True
15 **Orchestral Manoeuvres in the Dark** -
   If You Leave

16 **New Order** - Blue Monday
17 **Soft Cell** - Tainted Love
18 **Modern English** - I Melt with You
19 **Gary Numan** - Cars
20 **Dexys Midnight Runners** - Come On Eileen
21 **The Human League** - Don't You Want Me
22 **Violent Femmes** - Blister in the Sun
23 **The Bangles** - Walk Like An Egyptian
24 **Berlin** - The Metro
25 **Devo** - Whip It*
26 **Frankie Goes to Hollywood** - Relax
27 **INXS** - Need You Tonight
28 **Cyndi Lauper** - Girls Just Want to Have Fun
29 **The Psychedelic Furs** - Pretty in Pink
30 **Talk Talk** - It's My Life
31 **Simple Minds** - Don't You (Forget About Me)
32 **Toni Basil** - Mickey
33 **Nena** - *99 Luftballons*
34 **Sparks** - Angst in My Pants
35 **Tears for Fears** - Shout
36 **'Til Tuesday** - Voices Carry

37 **Romeo Void** - Never Say Never
38 **a-ha** - Take On Me

> \*   Mark Mothersbaugh has had a life after Devo as the
>     composer on the Wes Anderson films *Bottle Rocket*,
>     *Rushmore*, *The Royal Tenenbaums*, and *The Life Aquatic
>     with Steve Zissou*.

## OPERA

It really doesn't hurt to have a little knowledge of opera. It's not only fantastically dramatic music, but it'll also make you look smart and well-rounded—kind of like the people who sing it.

01 **Giacomo Puccini** - *Che gelida manina* from *La Bohème* (Jussi Björling, *Great Recordings of the Century: Puccini: La Bohème*)

02 **Georges Bizet** - *L'amour est un oiseau rebelle (Habanera)* from Act I of *Carmen* (Herbert von Karajan and the Vienna Philharmonic Orchestra, *Carmen: Extraits*)

03 **Amilcare Ponchielli** - Dance of the Hours from *La Gioconda* (Eugene Ormandy and the Philadelphia Orchestra, *The Fantastic Philadelphians*)

04 **Richard Wagner\*** - *Das Rheingold*: Entrance of the Gods Into Valhalla from *The Ring* (Slovak Radio Symphony Orchestra, *Wagner: The Ring (Orchestral Highlights)*)

05 **Richard Wagner** - *Wahn! Wahn! Überall Wahn!* from *Die Meistersinger von Nürnberg* (Bryn Terfel, Claudio Abbado, and the Berliner Philharmoniker, *Wagner: Opera Arias*)

06 **Richard Wagner** - *Die Walkure*: Ride of the Valkyries from *The Ring* (Slovak Radio Symphony Orchestra, *Wagner: The Ring (Orchestral Highlights)*)

07 **Richard Wagner** - *Die Walkure*: Wotan's Farewell and Magic Fire (Slovak Radio Symphony Orchestra, *Wagner: The Ring (Orchestral Highlights)*)

08 **Wolfgang Amadeus Mozart** - *Der Vogelfänger Bin Ich Ja (Papageno)* from *Die Zauberflöte* (Gottfried Hornik, Herbert von Karajan, and the Berliner Philharmoniker, *Mozart: Die Zauberflöte: Highlights*)

09 **Richard Wagner** - *Gotterdammerung*: Siegfried's Death and Funeral March (Slovak Radio Symphony Orchestra, *Wagner: The Ring (Orchestral Highlights)*)

10 **Ruggiero Leoncavallo** - *Vesti la giubba* from Act I of *I Pagliacci* (Jussi Björling, *Operatic Arias*)

11 **Vincenzo Bellini** - *Or dove fuggo io mai* from Act I, Scene 1, of *I Puritani* (Tullio Serafin, *Bellini: I Puritani*)

12 **Giuseppe Verdi** - *Manrico? . . . Di quella pira* from *Il Trovatore* (Daniela Longhi and the Hungarian State Opera Orchestra, *Best of Opera, Vol. 4*)

13 **Wolfgang Amadeus Mozart** - *Voi Che Sapete* from *Le Nozze di Figaro* (Anne-Sofie von Otter, James Levine, and the Metropolitan Opera Orchestra, *Mozart: Le Nozze di Figaro: Highlights*)

14 **Giacomo Puccini** - *Coro a bocca chiusa* from Act II
of *Madame Butterfly* (Humming Chorus) (Herbert
von Karajan and the Chor der Wiener Staatsoper and
Wiener Philharmonike, *Puccini: Madame Butterfly*)

15 **Giacomo Puccini** - *Un bel dì vedremo* from
*Madame Butterfly* (Mirella Freni, Herbert von
Karajan, and the Wiener Philharmoniker, *The
Ultimate Puccini Divas Album*)

16 **Vincenzo Bellini** - *Casta Diva* from *Norma*
(Renée Fleming, Sir Charles Mackerras, and the
London Philharmonic Orchestra and London
Voices, *Renée Fleming*)

17 **Giacomo Puccini** - *O mio babbino caro* from
*Madame Butterfly* (André Rieu, *Tuscany*)

18 **Richard Wagner** - Prelude from Act III of *Die
Meistersinger von Nürnberg* (Leopold Stokowski
and the Royal Philharmonic Orchestra, *Wagner:
Orchestral Works*)

19 **Giuseppe Verdi** - *La donna é mobile* from *Rigoletto*
(Luciano Pavarotti, Richard Bonynge, and the
London Symphony Orchestra, *The Essential Pavarotti*)

20 **George Frideric Handel** - *Armida dispietata . . .
Lascia ch'io pianga mia cruda sorte* from *Rinaldo*
(Renée Fleming, Harry Bicket, and the Orchestra

of the Age of Enlightenment, *Handel Arias*)

21 **George Frideric Handel** - *Ombra mai fu "Largo"* from *Serse* (Renée Fleming, Harry Bicket, and the Orchestra of the Age of Enlightenment, *Handel Arias*)

22 **Giacomo Puccini** - *E Lucevan le Stelle* from *Tosca* (Plácido Domingo, Giuseppe Sinopoli, and the Philharmonia Orchestra, *Granada: The Greatest Hits of Plácido Domingo*)

23 **Richard Wagner** - *Mild und Leise (Isoldes Liebestod)* from *Tristan und Isolde* (Jessye Norman, Sir Colin Davis, and the London Symphony Orchestra, *The Essential Jessye Norman*)

24 **Richard Wagner** - Prelude from Act I of *Tristan und Isolde* (Berliner Philharmoniker, *Tristan und Isolde*)

25 **Giacomo Puccini** - *Nessum dorma!* from *Turandot* (Luciano Pavarotti, *The Three Tenors In Concert*)

---

\*   While Wagner is considered to be one of the greatest composers of all time, I would just like to point out that he's also considered one of the biggest inspirations to Adolf Hitler—not musically, but genocidally. His music was often played as Jews and other inhabitants of World War II death camps went to be executed.

## POP PUNK

Sex Pistols a little too scary and dirty for you?
Fear not, pop punk is here.

01 **blink-182** - All the Small Things
02 **Weezer** - Buddy Holly
03 **The Donnas** - Skintight
04 **Good Charlotte** - Lifestyles of the Rich and Famous
05 **Taking Back Sunday** - A Decade Under the Influence
06 **My Chemical Romance** - I'm Not Okay (I Promise)
07 **The Used** - The Taste of Ink
08 **New Found Glory** - My Friends Over You
09 **Saves the Day** - At Your Funeral
10 **Jimmy Eat World** - The Middle
11 **Green Day** - Basket Case
12 **Sum41** - Fat Lip
13 **AFI** - Girl's Not Grey
14 **Something Corporate** - Space
15 **Story of the Year** - Until the Day I Die
16 **Goldfinger** - My Head
17 **The Bouncing Souls** - True Believers

**ESSENTIAL GENRES**

18 **Less Than Jake** - Look What Happened

19 **The Get Up Kids** - I'm a Loner Dottie, a Rebel

20 **NOFX** - Bob

21 **Simple Plan** - Perfect

22 **Brand New** - Seventy Times 7

23 **The Living End** - Second Solution

24 **Unwritten Law** - Seein' Red

25 **The Offspring** - Come Out and Play

## THE POP TARTS

Life wasn't always about Swedish production teams manufacturing pop music by the busload. Thank God it is now.

01 **\*NSYNC** - Bye Bye Bye
02 **Christina Aguilera** - Genie in a Bottle
03 **\*NSYNC** - Tearin' Up My Heart
04 **Britney Spears** - Baby One More Time
05 **Backstreet Boys** - Everybody (Backstreet's Back)
06 **Debbie Gibson** - Electric Youth
07 **Britney Spears** - Toxic
08 **New Kids on the Block** - You Got It (The Right Stuff)
09 **Justin Timberlake** - Like I Love You
10 **Christina Aguilera** - Beautiful
11 **Backstreet Boys** - I Want It That Way
12 **\*NSYNC** - Pop
13 **Christina Aguilera** - What a Girl Wants
14 **LFO** - Summer Girls
15 **98 Degrees** - I Do (Cherish You)
16 **Take That** - Back for Good
17 **New Kids on the Block** - Hangin' Tough

18 **Backstreet Boys** - Quit Playing Games (With My Heart)

19 **New Edition** - Cool It Now

20 **Justin Timberlake** - Cry Me a River

21 **Menudo** - Hold Me

22 **Kylie Minogue** - Loco-Motion

23 **Mandy Moore** - Candy

## PUNK SONGS

Punk is such a debatable concept. What is punk? What is punk rock? Finding a defining term that everyone can agree on is not only impossible, it's also not very punk rock. What people might agree on is that these are songs every punk rocker should at least know.

01 **The Clash** - London Calling
02 **Dead Kennedys** - California Über Alles
03 **Black Flag** - Rise Above
04 **Hüsker Dü** - Something I Learned Today
05 **Rancid** - Ruby Soho
06 **Sex Pistols** - God Save the Queen
07 **Bad Brains** - I Against I
08 **Dead Kennedys** - Holiday in Cambodia
09 **Ramones** - I Wanna Be Sedated
10 **MC5** - Kick Out the Jams
11 **Agent Orange** - Too Young to Die
12 **Reagan Youth** - Degenerated
13 **The Stooges** - I Wanna Be Your Dog
14 **Bad Religion** - Stranger Than Fiction
15 **Public Image Ltd.** - Rise
16 **The Clash** - I Fought the Law

ESSENTIAL GENRES

17 **Fugazi** - Waiting Room
18 **The Dead Milkmen** - Punk Rock Girl
19 **NOFX** - Linoleum
20 **Sex Pistols** - Anarchy in the U.K.

ESSENTIAL GENRES

## R & B

R & B is soothing and sexy and smooth. It's about heartbreak and longing, and it's always good to play when you're trying to win over someone's affections. These aren't classics, and these aren't the most recent cuts, but these are songs that you probably know and love.

01 **Lauryn Hill** - Doo Wop (That Thing)
02 **Alicia Keys** - Fallin'
03 **Erykah Badu** - On & On
04 **Mary J. Blige** - Real Love
05 **Montell Jordan** - This Is How We Do It
06 **Aaliyah** - Rock the Boat*
07 **Toni Braxton** - Un-Break My Heart
08 **D'Angelo** - Untitled (How Does It Feel)
09 **Terence Trent D'Arby** - Wishing Well
10 **Usher** - Yeah!
11 **Boys II Men** - End of the Road
12 **TLC** - Waterfalls
13 **All-4-One** - I Swear
14 **Color Me Badd** - I Adore Mi Amor
15 **SWV** - Weak
16 **Bell Biv DeVoe** - Do Me!

ESSENTIAL GENRES

17 **Justin Timberlake** - Like I Love You
18 **Craig David** - Fill Me In
19 **Brandy and Monica** - The Boy Is Mine
20 **Whitney Houston** - Saving All My Love
   For You
21 **R. Kelly** - I Believe I Can Fly

\*   Aaliyah, who died in a plane crash in the Bahamas in
    2001, married fellow R & B singer R. Kelly when she
    was an underage teenager, though the marriage was
    annulled just weeks later when her family found out.

## REGGAE

Reggae is one of those timeless genres—many of the songs made today sound like they were made twenty years ago, and vice versa. Its influences can be heard in a lot of other genres of music, including goth.

01 **Max Romeo** - Chase the Devil
02 **Augustus Pablo** - Stop Them Jah
03 **Israel Vibration** - The Same Song*
04 **John Holt** - Ali Baba
05 **Horace Andy** - Nice and Easy
06 **Althia and Donna** - Uptown Top Ranking
07 **Barrington Levy** - Murderer
08 **Capleton** - Jah Jah City
09 **Lee "Scratch" Perry** - Soul Fire**
10 **Prince Buster** - Al Capone
11 **Dawn Penn** - You Don't Love Me (No, No, No)
12 **Junior Murvin** - Police and Thieves
13 **The Congos** - Rock of Gibraltar
14 **Ossie Delamore** - Time Has Come
15 **Culture** - Babylon Can't Study
16 **Toots and the Maytals** - Pressure Drop
17 **Shaggy** - Boombastic

18 **Shabba Ranks** - Mr. Loverman
19 **The Melodians** - Rivers of Babylon
20 **Dennis Brown** - Wildfire
21 **Peter Tosh** - Legalize it
22 **Bunny Wailer** - Amagideon (Armageddon)
23 **The Twinkle Brothers** - Never Get Burn
24 **Niney the Observer** - Blood and Fire
25 **Tenor Saw** - Ring the Alarm
26 **Anthony Redrose** - Tempo
27 **Barrington Levy** - Here I Come
28 **King Tubby** - Fittest of the Fittest
29 **Jimmy Cliff** - Many Rivers to Cross***
30 **Bob Marley** - Redemption Song

---

\*    The three vocalists in Israel Vibration—Cecil "Skeleton" Spence, Albert "Apple Gabriel" Craig, and Lascelle "Wiss" Bulgin—met in a polio clinic in Kingston, Jamaica.

\*\*    Legendary producer Lee Perry built Black Ark Studios in 1974 and recorded some of the greatest, most innovative reggae of all time, including Bob Marley and the Wailers' first record. Often described as a madman and a genius, Perry's erratic behavior culminated in his trashing and burning the studio down in 1979.

\*\*\*    Jimmy Cliff starred in 1973's *The Harder They Come* as a renegade Kingston singer who becomes a modern-day Robin Hood.

## SHOW TUNES

Whether you're preparing for your school musical or just trying to fit in with the drama kids, it's always good to be overheard singing any of these gems. Plus, they're totally fun.

**ESSENTIAL GENRES**

01 **All That Jazz** - *Chicago*
02 **Welcome to My Party** - *The Wild Party*
03 **Out Tonight** - *Rent*
04 **Don't Tell Mama** - *Cabaret*
05 **Big Spender** - *Sweet Charity*
06 **Touch-A, Touch-A, Touch Me** - *The Rocky Horror Picture Show*
07 **Greased Lightnin'** - *Grease*
08 **I Could Have Danced All Night** - *My Fair Lady*
09 **One Last Kiss** - *Bye Bye Birdie*
10 **Origin of Love** - *Hedwig and the Angry Inch*
11 **The Last Night of the World** - *Miss Saigon*
12 **Edelweiss** - *The Sound of Music*
13 **Oh, What A Beautiful Mornin'** - *Oklahoma!*
14 **I Feel Pretty** - *West Side Story*
15 **Consider Yourself** - *Oliver!*
16 **A Bushel and a Peck** - *Guys and Dolls*
17 **Can't Help Lovin' Dat Man** - *Show Boat*

## SOUL

There's a saying that goes, "You don't know where you're going unless you know where you came from." That perfectly describes soul music.

01 **The Marvelettes** - Too Many Fish in the Sea
02 **The Four Tops** - Baby I Need Your Loving
03 **The Contours** - Do You Love Me
04 **Jimmy Ruffin** - What Becomes of the Brokenhearted
05 **Ronnie Spector** - Lovely Laddy Day
06 **Barrett Strong** - Money (That's What I want)
07 **Eddie Holland** - Leaving Here
08 **Marvin Gaye** - How Sweet It Is (To Be Loved by You)
09 **The Contours** - First I Look at the Purse
10 **Barbara McNair** - It Happens Every Time
11 **Frank Wilson** - 'Til You Were Gone
12 **The Miracles** - Shop Around
13 **The Four Tops** - It's the Same Old Song
14 **The Supremes** - You Can't Hurry Love
15 **The Temptations** - Ain't Too Proud to Beg
16 **Tammi Terrell** - I Gotta Find a Way to Get You Back

17 **Jackson 5** - I Want You Back

18 **The Marvelettes** - Please Mr. Postman

19 **Smokey Robinson and the Miracles** - Tears of a Clown

20 **The Commodores** - Easy

21 **Chris Clark** - Do I Love You

22 **Jackson 5** - I'll be There

23 **Stevie Wonder** - Uptight (Everything's Alright)

24 **Martha and the Vandellas** - Nowhere to Run

25 **Roy Ayers** - Everybody Loves the Sunshine

## TECHNO

Eminem might have declared techno dead in one of his songs, but he had no idea what he was talking about. It's alive and well and still beating. Playlist by DJ Tera.

ESSENTIAL GENRES

01 **Derrick May** - Strings of Life
02 **Joey Beltram** - Energy Flash
03 **Reese** - Rock to the Beat
04 **Underground Resistance** - The Seawolf
05 **Cybotron** - Clear
06 **The Project** - Do That Dance
07 **A Homeboy, a Hippie & a Funki Dredd** - Total Confusion
08 **Frankie Bones** - Call It Techno
09 **LFO** - LFO
10 **Polygon Window** - Polygon Window
11 **Basic Channel** - Phylyps Trak
12 **Jeff Mills** - Late Night
13 **Brother From Another Planet** - Planet Earth
14 **Tronik House** - Mental Techno
15 **Vainqueur** - Vainqueur (Maurizio Mix)
16 **DBX** - Losing Control

17 **Dave Clarke** - Red 1
18 **Tricky Disco** - House Fly
19 **Renegade Soundwave** - The Phantom
20 **Juno** - Soul Thunder

# >> ESSENTIAL ARTISTS >>

## MENU

# >> ESSENTIAL ARTISTS >>

There are certain artists whose work is essential to anyone's music library. Some musicians and their songs are constantly referenced in popular culture, and some of these performers have had a profound influence on music. From Elvis to Eminem and everything in between, here are some essential artists and the best tunes from each of their collections.

## 2PAC

01 **I Ain't Mad at Cha** - *All Eyez on Me*
02 **Dear Mama** - *Me Against the World*
03 **Keep Ya Head Up** - *Strictly 4 My N.I.G.G.A.Z.*
04 **Old School** - *Me Against the World*
05 **Temptations** - *Me Against the World*
06 **So Many Tears** - *Me Against the World*
07 **If I Die 2 Nite** - *Me Against the World*
08 **Me Against the World** - *Me Against the World*
09 **Krazy** - *The Don Killuminati: The 7 Day Theory*
10 **Hail Mary** - *The Don Killuminati: The 7 Day Theory*
11 **Toss It Up** - *The Don Killuminati: The 7 Day Theory*
12 **Me and My Girlfriend** - *The Don Killuminati: The 7 Day Theory*
13 **Holler if Ya Hear Me** - *Strictly 4 My N.I.G.G.A.Z.*
14 **I Get Around** - *Strictly 4 My N.I.G.G.A.Z.*
15 **Pour Out a Little Liquor** - soundtrack to *Above the Rim*

16 **Do 4 Love** - *R U Still Down? (Remember Me)*
17 **2 of Amerika's Most Wanted** (featuring Snoop
   Dogg) - *All Eyez on Me*

> Tupac Amaru Shakur's birth name was Lesane Parish Crooks.

> 2Pac was gunned down in Las Vegas after a long-standing
  dispute with hip-hop rival Biggie Small, who was shot and
  killed shortly after. The early death of 2Pac turned him into an
  unlikely prophet, since many of his songs were about dying,
  death, getting shot . . . you know, the warm and fuzzy stuff.

> 2Pac was in the Digital Underground.

> 2Pac studied drama at the Baltimore School for the Arts.

◀)) **If you like this, you might also like:**
**The Notorious B.I.G., N.W.A., Ja Rule, DMX.**

## AC/DC

01 **You Shook Me All Night Long** - *Back in Black*
02 **Dirty Deeds Done Dirt Cheap** - *Dirty Deeds Done Dirt Cheap*
03 **Back in Black** - *Back in Black*
04 **Touch Too Much** - *Highway to Hell*
05 **It's a Long Way to the Top (If You Wanna Rock 'N' Roll)** - *T.N.T.*
06 **Let's Get it Up** - *For Those About to Rock*
07 **Who Made Who** - *Who Made Who*
08 **Hells Bells** - *Back in Black*
09 **Moneytalks** - *The Razor's Edge*
10 **Flick of the Switch** - *Flick of the Switch*
11 **Guns for Hire** - *Flick of the Switch*
12 **Thunderstruck** - *The Razor's Edge*
13 **For Those About To Rock (We Salute You)** - *For Those About to Rock*
14 **Shoot to Thrill** - *Back in Black*
15 **Whole Lotta Rosie** - *Let There Be Rock*
16 **Let There Be Rock** - *Let There Be Rock*
17 **The Jack** - *T.N.T.*
18 **Mistress for Christmas** - *The Razor's Edge*
19 **Evil Walks** - *For Those About to Rock*

ESSENTIAL ARTISTS

20 **T.N.T.** - *T.N.T.*
21 **Highway to Hell** - *Highway to Hell*
22 **Bad Boy Boogie** - *Let There Be Rock*
23 **High Voltage** - *T.N.T.*
24 **Sin City** - *Powerage*

> Original AC/DC vocalist Bon Scott drank himself to death on February 20, 1980, at the age of thirty-three.

> Guitarist Angus Young was only fifteen years old when he started in AC/DC. As a result, one of AC/DC's signature looks was Young's school uniform, which he wore on stage.

🔊 **If you like this, you might also like:**
**Jet, Thin Lizzy, the Who.**

ESSENTIAL ARTISTS

## THE BEACH BOYS

01 **Surfin' Safari** - *Surfin' Safari*
02 **Surfin' USA** - *Surfin' USA*
03 **Little Deuce Coupe** - *Surfer Girl*
04 **Fun, Fun, Fun** - *Shut Down Volume 2*
05 **I Get Around** - *All Summer Long*
06 **Do You Wanna Dance** - *Today!*
07 **Help Me, Rhonda** - *Today!*
08 **California Girls** - *Summer Days (and Summer Nights!!)*
09 **Barbara Ann** - *Beach Boys' Party!*
10 **Sloop John B** - *Pet Sounds*
11 **Wouldn't It Be Nice** - *Pet Sounds*
12 **Caroline No** - *Pet Sounds*
13 **Hang On to Your Ego** - *Pet Sounds*
14 **Good Vibrations** - *Smiley Smile*
15 **409** - *Surfin' Safari*
16 **Don't Worry Baby** - *Shut Down Volume 2*
17 **God Only Knows** - *Pet Sounds*
18 **Catch a Wave** - *Surfer Girl*
19 **Kokomo** - soundtrack to *Cocktail*

123

> Mass murderer Charles Manson lived for a while with Dennis Wilson, and the Beach Boys even recorded a song rumored to have been written by Manson, "Never Learn Not to Love," on the album *20/20*.

> The band's first number one single was "I Get Around."

> The band's original name was the Pendletones; other early names included "Kenny and the Cadets" and "Carl and the Passions."

◀)) If you like this, you might also like: Weezer, the Turtles, the Zombies, the Monkees, acoustic songs by the Vines.

ESSENTIAL ARTISTS

## BEASTIE BOYS

ESSENTIAL ARTISTS

125

22 **The Move** - *Hello Nasty*
23 **Hey Ladies** - *Paul's Boutique*

> The real names of the Beastie Boys: Michael Diamond (Mike D), Adam Yauch (MCA), and Adam Horovitz (Adrock).

> The Beastie Boys were originally a hardcore band.

> The Beastie Boys were the opening band for Madonna's Virgin tour in 1985.

◀)) **If you like this, you might also like: Biz Markie, Beck, 311, House of Pain, the Roots.**

## THE BEATLES

01 **Twist and Shout** - *Please Please Me*
02 **Love Me Do** - *Please Please Me*
03 **You've Got to Hide Your Love Away** - *Help!*
04 **Yellow Submarine** - *Yellow Submarine*
05 **A Hard Day's Night** - *A Hard Day's Night*
06 **Help!** - *Help!*
07 **Hey Jude** - *The Beatles 1*
08 **I Want to Hold Your Hand** - *Meet the Beatles!*
09 **Across the Universe** - *Let It Be*
10 **Dear Prudence** - *The Beatles (The White Album)*
11 **Can't Buy Me Love** - *A Hard Day's Night*
12 **Drive My Car** - *Rubber Soul*
13 **Let It Be** - *Let It Be*
14 **Money (That's What I Want)** - *With the Beatles*
15 **Baby You're a Rich Man** - *Magical Mystery Tour*
16 **Revolution** - *Hey Jude*
17 **Sexy Sadie** - *The Beatles (The White Album)*
18 **Something** - *Abbey Road*
19 **In My Life** - *Rubber Soul*
20 **I Saw Her Standing There** - *Please Please Me*
21 **All Together Now** - *Yellow Submarine*
22 **All You Need Is Love** - *Magical Mystery Tour*

ESSENTIAL ARTISTS

> The song "Eleanor Rigby" has been recorded by Diana Ross and the Supremes, Paul Anka, Frankie Valli, the Four Tops, Ray Charles, and Aretha Franklin, among many others.

> "Hey Jude" was written by Paul McCartney for John Lennon's son Julian.

> It's believed that the song "Lucy in the Sky with Diamonds" is a reference to the psychedelic drug LSD. However, it's also been said that the name is in reference to how Lennon's son Julian described a painting he made in school.

🔊 If you like this, you might also like: the Kinks, the Libertines, the Lilys, the Strokes, and every band since the Beatles broke up.

## BECK

01 **Loser** - *Mellow Gold*
02 **Beercan** - *Mellow Gold*
03 **Pay No Mind (Snoozer)** - *Mellow Gold*
04 **Fuckin with My Head** - *Mellow Gold*
05 **Fume** - *Loser UK EP*
06 **Soul Suckin Jerk (Reject)** - *Loser UK EP*
07 **Debra** - *Midnite Vultures*
08 **Peaches & Cream** - *Midnite Vultures*
09 **Sexx Laws** - *Midnite Vultures*
10 **Nobody's Fault But My Own** - *Mutations*
11 **Tropicalia** - *Mutations*
12 **Devils Haircut** - *Odelay*
13 **The New Pollution** - *Odelay*
14 **Where It's At** - *Odelay*
15 **Novacane** - *Odelay*
16 **Jack-ass** - *Odelay*
17 **The Golden Age** - *Sea Change*
18 **Sunday Sun** - *Sea Change*
19 **Lonesome Tears** - *Sea Change*
20 **Guess I'm Doing Fine** - *Sea Change*
21 **Lost Cause** - *Sea Change*
22 **E-Pro** - *Guero*

**ESSENTIAL ARTISTS**

> Beck is a practicing Scientologist.

> Beck once recorded a song called "MTV Makes Me Want to Smoke Crack."

> Beck was born Beck David Campbell, but took his mother's maiden name, Hansen.

🔊 **If you like this, you might also like: Jon Spencer Blues Explosion, Folk Implosion, Ima Robot, Cornershop.**

ESSENTIAL ARTISTS

## BJÖRK

01 **Big Time Sensuality** - *Debut*
02 **Army of Me** - *Post*
03 **It's Oh So Quiet** - *Post*
04 **Human Behaviour** - *Debut*
05 **I Miss You** - *Post*
06 **Hyper-Ballad** - *Post*
07 **Possibly Maybe** - *Post*
08 **Isobel** - *Post*
09 **Violently Happy** - *Debut*
10 **Hunter** - *Homogenic*
11 **Joga** - *Homogenic*
12 **All Is Full of Love** - *Homogenic*
13 **Hidden Place** - *Vespertine*
14 **Pagan Poetry** - *Vespertine*
15 **I've Seen It All** (featuring Thom Yorke) -
   *Selmasong*
16 **The Modern Things** - *Post*
17 **Venus as a Boy** - *Debut*
18 **I Miss You** - *Telegram*
19 **Pleasure Is All Mine** - *Medulla*

ESSENTIAL ARTISTS

> Björk is from Iceland and was a child star in her native country, releasing her first record at the age of eleven.

> Björk was originally in a band called the Sugarcubes and released her first solo album in 1993.

> Björk starred in the movie *Dancer in the Dark* (2000) and gave a critically acclaimed performance.

🔊 **If you like this, you might also like: Massive Attack, the Sneaker Pimps, Portishead, Denali, Primal Scream, Sigur Rós.**

ESSENTIAL ARTISTS

# BLONDIE

01 **Atomic** - *Eat to the Beat*
02 **Picture This** - *Parallel Lines*
03 **Hanging on the Telephone** - *Parallel Lines*
04 **Screaming Skin** - *No Exit*
05 **The Tide Is High** - *Autoamerican*
06 **Here's Looking at You** - *Autoamerican*
07 **Sunday Girl** - *Parallel Lines*
08 **Maria** - *No Exit*
09 **Call Me** - *Greatest Hits*
10 **Rapture** - *Autoamerican*
11 **Heart of Glass** - *Parallel Lines*
12 **One Way or Another** - *Parallel Lines*
13 **Slow Motion** - *Eat to the Beat*
14 **(I'm Always Touched By Your) Presence Dear** - *Plastic Letters*
15 **Dreaming** - *Eat to the Beat*

ESSENTIAL ARTISTS

> With origins in the New York City punk-rock scene and acceptance in the Studio 54 disco scene, Blondie brought together two worlds that couldn't have been more different.

> Blondie's singer, Debbie Harry, was once a Playboy bunny.

> Debbie Harry and guitarist Chris Stein were once a couple.

> Blondie got its name from the catcalls Debbie Harry used to hear on the street.

🔊 **If you like this, you might also like: Franz Ferdinand, the Ramones, Berlin, Elastica, the Yeah Yeah Yeahs, early Blur.**

# BLUR

01 **Song 2** - *Blur*
02 **Girls & Boys** - *Parklife*
03 **End of a Century** - *Parklife*
04 **Charmless Man** - *The Great Escape*
05 **There's No Other Way** - *Leisure*
06 **Out of Time** - *Think Tank*
07 **Tender** - *13*
08 **Coffee & TV** - *13*
09 **Beetlebum** - *Blur*
10 **Battery in Your Leg** - *Think Tank*
11 **Magic America** - *Parklife*
12 **Pop Scene** - *Modern Life Is Rubbish*
13 **Death of a Party** - *Blur*
14 **She's So High** - *Leisure*
15 **The Universal** - *The Great Escape*
16 **Ambulance** - *Think Tank*
17 **This Is a Low** - *Parklife*
18 **Country House** - *The Great Escape*
19 **To the End** - *Parklife*
20 **Parklife** - *Parklife*
21 **Crazy Beat** - *Think Tank*

> Blur's singer, Damon Albarn, used to be in a relationship with Elastica's singer, Justine Frischmann. It is believed that Blur's album *13* was about the decline of their relationship.

> Damon Albarn is also the lead singer of Gorillaz.

> In 2002 original Blur guitarist Graham Coxon left the band.

🔊 **If you like this, you might also like: Elastica, Gorillaz, Oasis, Pulp, the Stone Roses, Supergrass, Razorlight, Kaiser Chiefs.**

## DAVID BOWIE

01 **Heroes** - *Heroes*
02 **Space Oddity** - *Space Oddity*
03 **The Man Who Sold the World** - *The Man Who Sold the World*
04 **Changes** - *Hunky Dory*
05 **John, I'm Only Dancing** - *The Rise and Fall of Ziggy Stardust and the Spiders from Mars*
06 **Ziggy Stardust** - *The Rise and Fall of Ziggy Stardust and the Spiders from Mars*
07 **Ashes to Ashes** - *Scary Monsters*
08 **Rebel Rebel** - *Diamond Dogs*
09 **Suffragette City** - *The Rise and Fall of Ziggy Stardust and the Spiders from Mars*
10 **I'm Afraid of Americans** - *Earthling*
11 **Jean Genie** - *Aladdin Sane*
12 **Aladdin Sane** - *Aladdin Sane*
13 **All the Young Dudes** - *Aladdin Sane (30th Anniversary Edition)*
14 **Let's Spend the Night Together** - *Aladdin Sane*
15 **Life on Mars?** - *Hunky Dory*
16 **Diamond Dogs** - *Diamond Dogs*

ESSENTIAL ARTISTS

17 **Fame** - *Young Americans*

18 **Golden Years** -*Station to Station*

19 **Fashion** - *Scary Monsters*

20 **Let's Dance** - *Let's Dance*

21 **China Girl** - *Let's Dance*

22 **Under Pressure** (featuring Queen) - *Best of Bowie*

23 **Station to Station** - *Station to Station*

24 **Cracked Actor** - *Aladdin Sane*

ESSENTIAL ARTISTS

> David Bowie's real name is David Robert Jones, but he changed it so as not to be confused with Monkees singer Davy Jones. His last name was taken from the name of the hunting knife.

> David Bowie had an alter ego named Ziggy Stardust, which he killed off during a concert at the Hammersmith Odeon in 1973.

> After being hit in the eye during a fight with schoolmate George Underwood, Bowie's pupil became paralyzed and was unable to contract, making that eye appear a different color from the other.

🔊 **If you like this, you might also like: Iggy Pop, Roxy Music, Pulp, Marilyn Manson's *Mechanical Animals*, the Killers, T. Rex, the New York Dolls, Queen.**

## BRIGHT EYES

01 **One Foot in Front of the Other** - compilation album *Saddle Creek 50*

02 **Something Vague** - *Fevers and Mirrors*

03 **I Must Belong Somewhere** - unreleased, available online

04 **Lover I Don't Have to Love** - *Lifted or the Story Is in the Soil, Keep Your Ear to the Ground*

05 **Let's Not Shit Ourselves (To Love and Be Loved)** - *Lifted or the Story Is in the Soil, Keep Your Ear to the Ground*

06 **Poison Oak** - *I'm Wide Awake, It's Morning*

07 **Lua** - *I'm Wide Awake, It's Morning*

08 **First Day of My Life** - *I'm Wide Awake, It's Morning*

09 **Road to Joy** - *I'm Wide Awake, It's Morning*

10 **Landlocked Blues** (featuring Emmylou Harris) - *I'm Wide Awake, It's Morning*

11 **The Calendar Hung Itself** - *Fevers and Mirrors*

12 **Hit the Switch** (featuring Nick Zinner) - *Digital Ash in a Digital Urn*

13 **I Woke Up With This Song in My Head This Morning** - *Lua*

14 **Nothing Gets Crossed Out** - *Lifted or the Story Is in the Soil, Keep Your Ear to the Ground*

15 **You Will. You? Will. You? Will. You? Will.** - *Lifted or the Story Is in the Soil, Keep Your Ear to the Ground*

16 **Method Acting** - *Lifted or the Story Is in the Soil, Keep Your Ear to the Ground*

17 **Take it Easy (Love Nothing)** - *Digital Ash in a Digital Urn*

18 **At The Bottom of Everything** (featuring Jim James) - *I'm Wide Awake, It's Morning*

19 **A Song to Pass the Time** - *Fevers and Mirrors*

> Conor Oberst is Bright Eyes.

> Oberst started releasing music in 1994, at the age of fourteen.

> Conor Oberst started the Saddle Creek label with friends and has since released albums from several artists, including the Faint.

🔊 **If you like this, you might also like: Cursive, the Decemberists, Bob Dylan, Johnathan Rice, Rilo Kiley.**

ESSENTIAL ARTISTS

## JAMES BROWN

01 **Get Up Offa That Thing** - *Papa's Got a Brand New Bag*
02 **Night Train [Closing]** - *Live at the Apollo [1963]*
03 **Cold Sweat** - *Cold Sweat*
04 **Funky President (People It's Bad)** - *Papa's Got a Brand New Bag*
05 **Think** - *Think*
06 **Get Up (I Feel Like Being A) Sex Machine** - *Sex Machine*
07 **I Got the Feelin'** - *Sex Machine*
08 **It's a Man's Man's Man's World** - *Sex Machine*
09 **Make It Funky** - *Revolution of the Mind*
10 **Mother Popcorn** - *Sex Machine*
11 **Papa's Got a Brand New Bag** - *Papa's Got a Brand New Bag*
12 **Please, Please, Please** - *Sex Machine*
13 **Soul Power** - *Revolution of the Mind*
14 **Super Bad** - *Revolution of the Mind*
15 **Try Me** - *Revolution of the Mind*
16 **(Do the) Mashed Potatoes** - *Soul Syndrome*
17 **Get on the Good Foot, Pts. 1 & 2** - *Get on the Good Foot*

ESSENTIAL ARTISTS

18 **Get It Together** - *Star Time*

19 **I Got You** - *Out of Sight*

20 **Papa Don't Take No Mess** - *Hell*

21 **Prisoner of Love** - *Prisoner of Love*

22 **Say It Loud (I'm Black and I'm Proud), Pts. 1 & 2** - *Say It Loud: I'm Black and I'm Proud*

23 **The Payback** - *The Payback*

> James Brown is also known as the "Godfather of Soul," "Soul Brother Number One," "Mr. Dynamite," and the "Hardest Working Man in Show Business."

🔊 **If you like this, you might also like: Aretha Franklin, Tina Turner, Ray Charles, Prince, Sly & the Family Stone.**

**ESSENTIAL ARTISTS**

142

## RAY CHARLES

01 **Here We Go Again** (duet with Norah Jones) - *Genius Loves Company*

02 **Hallelujah, I Love Her So** - *Ballad in Blue*

03 **Do I Ever Cross Your Mind?** (duet with Bonnie Raitt) - *Genius Loves Company*

04 **A Fool for You** - *In Concert*

05 **This Little Girl of Mine** - *Tell the Truth*

06 **Ain't That Love** - *The Birth of Soul*

07 **America the Beautiful** - *Anthology*

08 **Crying Time** - *Sweet & Sour Tears*

09 **Night Time Is the Right Time** - *The Genius Sings the Blues*

10 **Georgia on My Mind** - *The Genius Hits the Road*

11 **Hit the Road Jack** - *The Genius Hits the Road*

12 **I Got a Woman** - *Le Grand*

13 **Drown in My Own Tears** - *Sweet & Sour Tears*

14 **Lonely Avenue** - *The Right Time*

15 **It Should've Been Me** - *The Birth of Soul*

16 **Let's Go Get Stoned** - *Anthology*

17 **Unchain My Heart** - *Ballad in Blue*

18 **What'd I Say** - *The Best of Ray Charles: The Atlantic Years*

19 **Don't You Know** - *Ray, Rare and Live*

> Ray Charles was not born blind; he contracted a degenerative eye disease called glaucoma, which left him blind by age seven.

> While in Seattle, Washington, Ray Charles met the soon-to-be entrepreneur/performer Quincy Jones, and the two teenagers formed a combo, eventually landing small club and wedding gigs.

> Ray Charles's nickname was "the Genius."

ESSENTIAL ARTISTS

◀») **If you like this, you might also like: Nat King Cole, Stevie Wonder, Jerry Lee Lewis, James Brown, Quincy Jones, Norah Jones.**

## THE CHEMICAL BROTHERS

01 **It Began in Afrika** - *Come with Us*

02 **Galvanize** - *Push the Button*

03 **Hey Boy Hey Girl** - *Hey Boy Hey Girl*

04 **Out of Control** - *Surrender*

05 **Block Rockin' Beats** - *Dig Your Own Hole*

06 **Chemical Beats** - *Exit Planet Dust*

07 **Come With Us** - *Come With Us*

08 **Let Forever Be** - *Surrender*

09 **Setting Sun** - *Dig Your Own Hole*

10 **Dig Your Own Hole** - *Dig Your Own Hole*

11 **Dream On** - *Surrender*

12 **Jailbird** - compilation album *Chemical Reaction: The Best of British Electronica*

13 **Star Guitar** - *Come With Us*

14 **Asleep From Day** - *Surrender*

15 **The Test** - *Come With Us*

ESSENTIAL ARTISTS

> People who have appeared as guest vocalists on Chemical Brothers albums include Oasis's Noel Gallagher, the Verve's Richard Ashcroft, New Order's Bernard Sumner, Mazzy Star's Hope Sandoval, and Beth Orton.

🔊 **If you like this, you might also like: Fatboy Slim, Basement Jaxx, Daft Punk.**

## THE CLASH

01 **Clampdown** - *London Calling*
02 **Death or Glory** - *London Calling*
03 **I Fought the Law** - *The Clash*
04 **London Calling** - *London Calling*
05 **London's Burning** - *The Clash*
06 **Lost in the Supermarket** - *London Calling*
07 **This Is Radio Clash** - *This Is Radio Clash*
08 **Rock the Casbah** - *Combat Rock*
09 **Should I Stay or Should I Go** - *Combat Rock*
10 **Straight to Hell** - *Combat Rock*
11 **White Riot** - *The Clash*
12 **(White Man) In Hammersmith Palais** - *The Clash*
13 **Safe European Home** - *Give 'Em Enough Rope*
14 **Somebody Got Murdered** - *Sandinista!*
15 **The Magnificent Seven** - *Sandinista!*
16 **We Are The Clash** - *Cut the Crap*
17 **Police on My Back** - *Sandinista!*
18 **The Guns of Brixton** - *London Calling*
19 **Stay Free** - *Give 'Em Enough Rope*
20 **Tommy Gun** - *Give 'Em Enough Rope*

21 **Career Opportunities** - *The Clash*
22 **I'm Not Down** - *London Calling*
23 **I'm So Bored with the U.S.A.** - *The Clash*

> "(White Man) In Hammersmith Palais" is one of the best Clash songs and was written after Joe Strummer attended a reggae all-nighter at Hammersmith Palais and turned out to be the only white guy there.

> Joe Strummer was born John Graham Mellor. He and Mick Jones were both songwriters in the Clash.

> In 1983 Mick Jones was fired from the Clash and began his band Big Audio Dynamite, which had a hit with the song "The Globe."

◀)) **If you like this, you might also like: the Libertines, No Exit, the Undertones, Buzzcocks, Public Image Limited, the Jam.**

**ESSENTIAL ARTISTS**

147

## ELVIS COSTELLO

01 **Accidents Will Happen** - *Armed Forces*
02 **Alison** - *My Aim Is True*
03 **High Fidelity** - *Get Happy!!*
04 **Less Than Zero** - *My Aim Is True*
05 **Lipstick Vogue** - *This Year's Model*
06 **Man Out Of Time** - *Imperial Bedroom*
07 **Mystery Dance** - *My Aim Is True*
08 **New Amsterdam** - *Get Happy!!*
09 **Radio, Radio** - *Ten Bloody Marys & Ten How's Your Fathers*
10 **Veronica** - *Spike*
11 **Watching the Detectives** - *My Aim Is True*
12 **(The Angels Wanna Wear My) Red Shoes** - *My Aim Is True*
13 **I Want You** - *Blood and Chocolate*
14 **No Action** - *This Year's Model*
15 **Oliver's Army** - *Armed Forces*
16 **Pump It Up** - *This Year's Model*
17 **Everyday I Write the Book** - *Punch the Clock*
18 **Love For Tender** - *Get Happy!!*
19 **(What's So Funny 'Bout) Peace, Love and Understanding?** - *Armed Forces*

148

20 **You Little Fool** - *Imperial Bedroom*

21 **I Can't Stand Up (For Falling Down)** -
   *Get Happy!!*

> "High Fidelity" was the inspiration behind the title of the Nick Hornby novel of the same name, which was later turned into a movie starring John Cusack and Jack Black.

> "Less Than Zero" was the inspiration behind the title of the Bret Easton Ellis novel of the same name, which was later turned into a movie starring Andrew McCarthy and Robert Downey Jr.

> The performance of "Radio, Radio" on *Saturday Night Live* caused Costello to be banned from ever appearing on the late-night comedy show due to its lyrical content. This ban was later lifted.

ESSENTIAL ARTISTS

🔊 **If you like this, you might also like: the Jam, the Specials, the Beatles, XTC, the Clash, Ted Leo, early Joe Jackson, Graham Parker.**

## THE CURE

01 **2 Late** - *Lovesong*
02 **Breathe** - *Join the Dots: B-Sides & Rarities, 1978–2001*
03 **All Cats Are Grey** - . . . *Happily Ever After*
04 **Catch** - *Kiss Me, Kiss Me, Kiss Me*
05 **The Perfect Girl** - *Kiss Me, Kiss Me, Kiss Me*
06 **A Letter to Elise** - *Wish*
07 **Fascination Street** - *Fascination Street*
08 **Pictures of You** - *Disintegration*
09 **Charlotte Sometimes** - *Concert: The Cure Live*
10 **Boys Don't Cry** - *Boys Don't Cry*
11 **Just Like Heaven** - *Kiss Me, Kiss Me, Kiss Me*
12 **Push** - *The Head on the Door*
13 **In Between Days** - *The Head on the Door*
14 **Burn** - *Join the Dots: B-Sides & Rarities, 1978–2001*
15 **Halo** - *Friday I'm in Love*
16 **A Forest** - *Seventeen Seconds*
17 **Plainsong** - *Disintegration*
18 **Lovesong** - *Disintegration*
19 **A Night Like This** - *The Head on the Door*
20 **Close To Me** - *The Head on the Door*
21 **The Lovecats** - *Japanese Whispers*

> In 2004 the Cure hosted the traveling music festival called Curiosa, which featured such bands as Interpol, Muse, and the Cooper Temple Clause.

> The song "Killing an Arab" was inspired by the Albert Camus book *The Stranger*.

> The Cure are considered one of the innovators of goth music.

◀)) **If you like this, you might also like: Interpol, the Killers, the Smiths, Siouxsie and the Banshees, stellastarr*, Flesh for Lulu, Depeche Mode, Bauhaus, the Psychedelic Furs.**

**ESSENTIAL ARTISTS**

## DEPECHE MODE

01 **A Question of Lust** - *Black Celebration*
02 **Black Celebration** - *Black Celebration*
03 **Blasphemous Rumours** - *Some Great Reward*
04 **Enjoy the Silence** - *Violator*
05 **Everything Counts** - *Construction Time Again*
06 **I Feel You** - *Songs of Faith and Devotion*
07 **It's No Good** - *Ultra*
08 **Just Can't Get Enough** - *Speak and Spell*
09 **Master and Servant** - *Some Great Reward*
10 **People Are People** - *Some Great Reward*
11 **Personal Jesus** - *Violator*
12 **Policy of Truth** - *Violator*
13 **Puppets** - *Speak and Spell*

> Original band member Vince Clarke left Depeche Mode in 1982 to start Yazoo with Alison Moyet.

> In 1995 singer Dave Gahan, fueled by his addiction to heroin, attempted but failed to commit suicide.

> Martin Gore wrote most of Depeche Mode's songs.

◀)) **If you like this, you might also like: Orchestral Manoeuvres in the Dark, Pet Shop Boys, New Order, Spandau Ballet, Tears for Fears, a-ha, Erasure, and surprisingly, at times, Linkin Park.**

# NEIL DIAMOND

01 **America** - *The Jazz Singer*
02 **Cherry, Cherry** - *Just For You*
03 **Cracklin' Rosie** - *Tap Root Manuscript*
04 **Girl, You'll Be a Woman Soon** - *Just For You*
05 **He Ain't Heavy, He's My Brother** - *Tap Root Manuscript*
06 **I Am . . . I Said** - *Stones*
07 **I'm a Believer** - *Just for You*
08 **Love on the Rocks** - *The Jazz Singer*
09 **Red, Red Wine** - *Just For You*
10 **Heartlight** - *Heartlight*
11 **Sweet Caroline** - *Neil Diamond*
12 **Forever in Blue Jeans** - *You Don't Bring Me Flowers*
13 **Solitary Man** - *Just For You*
14 **Can You Feel the Love Tonight?** - *The Movie Album: As Time Goes By*
15 **Can't Help Falling in Love** - *The Movie Album: As Time Goes By*
16 **Havah Nagila** - *Live in America*
17 **Heaven Can Wait** - *In My Lifetime*
18 **Hello Again** - *The Jazz Singer*

**ESSENTIAL ARTISTS**

19 **Love Doesn't Live Here Anymore** - *Headed For the Future*

20 **Moon River** - *The Movie Album: As Time Goes By*

21 **The Little Drummer Boy** - *The Christmas Album*

22 **Unchained Melody** - *The Movie Album: As Time Goes By*

> Neil Diamond starred in a remake of *The Jazz Singer*.

> Neil Diamond's first number one hit was "Cherry, Cherry."

> Neil Diamond grew up in Brooklyn, New York, and attended the same high school as Barbra Streisand and Neil Sedaka.

🔊 **If you like this, you might also like: Pete Yorn, the Walkmen, Urge Overkill, Barbra Streisand.**

# THE DOORS

01 **People Are Strange** - *Strange Days*

02 **The Soft Parade** - *The Soft Parade*

03 **Peace Frog** - *Morrison Hotel*

04 **Love Me Two Times** - *Strange Days*

05 **Riders on the Storm** - *L.A. Woman*

06 **When the Music's Over** - *Strange Days*

07 **Love Street** - *Waiting for the Sun*

08 **Light My Fire** - *The Doors*

09 **The Crystal Ship** - *The Doors*

10 **Strange Days** - *Strange Days*

11 **Touch Me** - *The Soft Parade*

12 **Break on Through (to the Other Side)** - *The Doors*

13 **You're Lost Little Girl** - *Strange Days*

14 **Love Her Madly** - *L.A. Woman*

15 **Hello, I Love You** - *Waiting for the Sun*

16 **L.A. Woman** - *L.A. Woman*

17 **The End** - *The Doors*

ESSENTIAL ARTISTS

> Val Kilmer starred as Jim Morrison in the movie *The Doors*.

> Just like Kurt Cobain, Janis Joplin, and Jimi Hendrix, Jim Morrison died at the age of twenty-seven. His tombstone in Paris is almost as popular as any other tourist attraction in the city.

> Jim Morrison was arrested for indecent exposure, profanity, and drunkenness during a gig in Miami, Florida, in March 1969. He was sentenced to hard labor and fined, but he died before his legal problems were resolved.

> Echo & the Bunnymen covered the Doors' "People Are Strange" on the soundtrack for the movie *The Lost Boys*.

> In Radiohead's "Anyone Can Play Guitar," Thom Yorke sings about wanting to be Jim Morrison.

◀)) **If you like this, you might also like: Love, Jefferson Airplane, MC5, Pearl Jam, Elefant.**

ESSENTIAL ARTISTS

## DURAN DURAN

01 **A View to a Kill** - *Decade*

02 **Come Undone** - *The Wedding Album*

03 **Girls on Film** - *Duran Duran*

04 **Hungry Like the Wolf** - *Rio*

05 **Is There Something I Should Know?** - *Arena*

06 **New Moon on Monday** - *Seven and the Ragged Tiger*

07 **Notorious** - *Notorious*

08 **Ordinary World** - *The Wedding Album*

09 **Planet Earth** - *Duran Duran*

10 **Rio** - *Rio*

11 **Save a Prayer** - *Rio*

12 **The Reflex** - *Seven and the Ragged Tiger*

13 **Wild Boys** - *Arena*

14 **Perfect Day** - *Thank You*

15 **The Chauffeur** - *Rio*

16 **Electric Barbarella** - *Electric Barbarella*

17 **Union of the Snake** - *Seven and the Ragged Tiger*

18 **(Reach Up for the) Sunrise** - *Astronaut*

ESSENTIAL ARTISTS

> Three members of Duran Duran have the last name Taylor, but none of them are actually related.

> The name Duran Duran came from the evil villain character Durand-Durand in the movie *Barbarella*.

> Keyboardist Nick Rhodes's real last name is Bates, but it is rumored that he chose the name Rhodes after the keyboard he played on.

> In 1985 Simon LeBon, Nick Rhodes, and Roger Taylor formed the band Arcadia, while John Taylor and Andy Taylor formed Power Station.

🔊 If you like this, you might also like: Adam and the Ants, Modern English, the Human League, Orchestral Manoeuvres in the Dark, Blur, the Killers, the Bravery.

## BOB DYLAN

01 **Like a Rolling Stone** - *Highway 61 Revisited*
02 **Visions of Johanna** - *Blonde on Blonde*
03 **The Times They Are A-Changin'** - *The Times They Are A-Changin'*
04 **Girl of the North Country** - *The Freewheelin' Bob Dylan*
05 **It's Alright, Ma (I'm Only Bleeding)** - *Bringing It All Back Home*
06 **Desolation Row** - *Highway 61 Revisited*
07 **Just Like a Woman** - *Blonde on Blonde*
08 **Positively 4th Street** - *Bob Dylan's Greatest Hits*
09 **Sad-Eyed Lady of the Lowlands** - *Blonde on Blonde*
10 **Most Likely You Go Your Way and I'll Go Mine** - *Blonde on Blonde*
11 **Rainy Day Women #12 & 35** - *Blonde on Blonde*
12 **Tangled Up in Blue** - *Blood on the Tracks*
13 **One of Us Must Know (Sooner or Later)** - *Blonde on Blonde*
14 **If You See Her, Say Hello** - *Blood on the Tracks*
15 **Subterranean Homesick Blues** - *Bringing It All Back Home*
16 **Mr. Tambourine Man** - *Bringing It All Back Home*

ESSENTIAL ARTISTS

17 **It's All Over Now, Baby Blue** - *Bringing It All Back Home*

18 **All Along the Watchtower** - *John Wesley Harding*

19 **Lay, Lady, Lay** - *Nashville Skyline*

20 **It Ain't Me, Babe** - *Another Side of Bob Dylan*

21 **Tonight I'll Be Staying Here With You** - *Nashville Skyline*

22 **Masters of War** - *The Freewheelin' Bob Dylan*

23 **Blowin' in the Wind** - *The Freewhellin' Bob Dylan*

24 **Knockin' on Heaven's Door** - *Pat Garret & Billy the Kid*

25 **One More Cup of Coffee (Valley Below)** - *Desire*

26 **Love Sick** - *Love Sick*

27 **Boots of Spanish Leather** - *The Times They Are A-Changin'*

28 **Don't Think Twice, It's All Right** - *The Freewheelin' Bob Dylan*

29 **Gotta Serve Somebody** - *Slow Train Coming*

30 **Mississippi** - *Love and Theft*

> Bob Dylan was born Robert Allen Zimmerman. He took his last name from poet Dylan Thomas.

> Bob Dylan is the father of Wallflowers singer Jakob Dylan.

◀)) If you like this, you might also like: Bright Eyes, Joni Mitchell, Bruce Springsteen, Lou Reed, Jeff Buckley, Patti Smith, Tom Petty.

## EMINEM

01 **97' Bonnie & Clyde** - *The Slim Shady LP*
02 **Forgot About Dre** - Dr. Dre album *2001*
03 **Guilty Conscience** - *The Slim Shady LP*
04 **Just Don't Give a Fuck** - *The Slim Shady LP*
05 **My Name Is** - *The Slim Shady LP*
06 **Stan** (featuring Dido) - *The Marshall Mathers LP*
07 **The Real Slim Shady** - *The Marshall Mathers LP*
08 **The Way I Am** - *The Marshall Mathers LP*
09 **Lose Yourself** - soundtrack to *8 Mile*
10 **Mosh** - *Encore*
11 **Remember Me?** (featuring RBX and Sticky Fingaz) - *The Marshall Mathers LP*
12 **Role Model** - *The Slim Shady LP*
13 **Sing for the Moment** - *The Eminem Show*
14 **Soldier** - *The Eminem Show*
15 **White America** - *The Eminem Show*
16 **Without Me** - *Without Me*
17 **Purple Pills** - D12 EP *Purple Pills*
18 **Shit on You** - D12 EP *Purple Pills*
19 **Cum on Everybody** - *The Slim Shady LP*
20 **Kim** - *The Marshall Mathers LP*
21 **Like Toy Soldiers** - *Encore*

# The Pocket DJ

> Eminem was born Marshall Mathers.

> Eminem was a protégé of Dr. Dre.

> The cover of *The Slim Shady LP* alludes to Eminem dumping his ex-wife's body into a river.

> Eminem's daughter's name is Haley.

🔊 **If you like this, you might also like: Snoop Dogg, Dr. Dre, MC Chris, D12, Eazy-E, Wu-Tang Clan.**

## FLEETWOOD MAC

01 **Don't Stop** - *Rumours*
02 **Dreams** - *Rumours*
03 **Go Your Own Way** - *Rumours*
04 **Gypsy** - *Mirage*
05 **Landslide** - *Fleetwood Mac*
06 **Rhiannon** - *Fleetwood Mac*
07 **You Make Loving Fun** - *Rumours*
08 **As Long as You Follow** - *Greatest Hits*
09 **Little Lies** - *Tango in the Night*
10 **Monday Morning** - *Fleetwood Mac*
11 **Over & Over** - *Tusk*
12 **Sara** - *Tusk*
13 **World Turning** - *Fleetwood Mac*
14 **Think About Me** - *Tusk*
15 **Tusk** - *Tusk*
16 **Gold Dust Woman** - *Rumours*
17 **Edge of Seventeen** - Stevie Nicks solo album
   *Bella Donna*

ESSENTIAL ARTISTS

> The name Fleetwood Mac came from a Peter Green song that
  he named after Mick Fleetwood and John McVie, who also
  played with him on the 1996 recording.

> "Dreams" was the band's only song to reach number one in the USA.

> Peter Green of Fleetwood Mac was in the Bluesbreakers as a stand-in for Eric Clapton.

🔊 **If you like this, you might also like: the Eagles, Todd Rundgren, the Bangles, Sheryl Crow, Hole.**

ESSENTIAL ARTISTS

## MARVIN GAYE

01 **Ain't No Mountain High Enough** (duet with Tammi Terrell) - *Anthology*

02 **You're All I Need to Get By** - *Marvin Gaye & His Women*

03 **Mercy Mercy Me (The Ecology)** - *What's Going On*

04 **Sexual Healing** - *Midnight Love*

05 **Can I Get a Witness** - *Anthology*

06 **Got to Give It Up** - *Anthology*

07 **I Heard It Through the Grapevine** - *I Heard It Through the Grapevine*

08 **How Sweet It Is (to Be Loved by You)** - *How Sweet It Is to Be Loved by You*

09 **It Takes Two** (duet with Kim Weston) - *Marvin Gaye and His Girls*

10 **Let's Get It On** - *Let's Get It On*

11 **Little Darling (I Need You)** - *Moods of Marvin Gaye*

12 **Ain't That Peculiar** - *Moods of Marvin Gaye*

13 **Pride and Joy** - *On Stage Recorded Live*

14 **What's Going On** - *What's Going On*

ESSENTIAL ARTISTS

165

15 **When Did You Stop Loving Me, When Did I Stop Loving You** - *Here, My Dear*

16 **Ain't Nothing Like the Real Thing** (duet with Tammi Terrell) - *Marvin Gaye & Tammi Terrell: Greatest Hits*

> Marvin Gaye was tragically shot and killed by his own father a day before his forty-fifth birthday.

> It's scientifically proven that Marvin Gaye's voice puts people in the mood. (Okay, it's not really determined by science, but you get what I'm saying.)

> The album *Here, My Dear* was part of Gaye's divorce settlement from his then-wife, Anna Gordy. Ordered by a judge to turn over a large percentage of the profits from his next two albums to her, Marvin Gaye produced this bitter double album, laying bare the pain and sadness of the deterioration of their marriage.

🔊 **If you like this, you might also like: Nat King Cole, Smokey Robinson, Stevie Wonder, Seal, Terence Trent D'Arby, Al Green, Bill Withers.**

## THE GRATEFUL DEAD

01 **Mississippi Half-Step Uptown Toodeloo** - *Wake of the Flood*

02 **Eyes of the World** - *Wake of the Flood*

03 **Dark Star** - *Live/Dead*

04 **Sugaree** - *Steal Your Face*

05 **Crazy Fingers** - *Blues for Allah*

06 **Feel Like a Stranger** - *Go to Heaven*

07 **Sugar Magnolia** - *American Beauty*

08 **He's Gone** - *Europe '72*

09 **Scarlet Begonias** - *Grateful Dead from the Mars Hotel*

10 **The Music Never Stopped** - *Blues for Allah*

11 **One More Saturday Night** - *Europe '72*

12 **St. Stephen** - *Live/Dead*

13 **Unbroken Chain** - *Grateful Dead from the Mars Hotel*

14 **Viola Lee Blues** - *Grateful Dead*

15 **Help On the Way/Slipknot!** - *Blues for Allah*

16 **Franklin's Tower** - *Blues for Allah*

17 **Jack Straw** - *Europe '72*

18 **Tennessee Jed** - *Europe '72*

19 **Althea** - *Go to Heaven*

ESSENTIAL ARTISTS

20 **Stagger Lee** - *Shakedown Street*

21 **Estimated Prophet** - *Terrapin Station*

22 **Dire Wolf** - *Workingman's Dead*

23 **Jack-A-Roe** - *Reckoning*

24 **Box of Rain** - *American Beauty*

25 **Operator** - *American Beauty*

26 **Candyman** - *American Beauty*

27 **Cumberland Blues** - *Workingman's Dead*

28 **High Time** - *Workingman's Dead*

**ESSENTIAL ARTISTS**

> After dropping out of high school in 1959, Jerry Garcia enlisted in the army but was given a general discharge after nine months.

> Garcia's first public performance was at Sebastopol, California's Analy High School.

> Jerry Garcia lost part of the middle finger on his right hand at the age of four when his older brother accidentally chopped it off with an axe.

🔊 **If you like this, you might also like: Phish, String Cheese Incident, MOE.**

## GREEN DAY

01 **When I Come Around** - *Dookie*
02 **Rotting** - *Time of Your Life (Good Riddance)*
03 **Basket Case** - *Dookie*
04 **Longview** - *Dookie*
05 **Good Riddance (Time of Your Life)** - *Nimrod*
06 **Boulevard of Broken Dreams** - *American Idiot*
07 **Suffocate** - *Time of Your Life (Good Riddance)*
08 **American Idiot** - *American Idiot*
09 **Nice Guys Finish Last** - *Nimrod*
10 **Minority** - *Warning*
11 **Platypus (I Hate You)** - *Nimrod*
12 **Welcome to Paradise** - *Dookie*
13 **80** - *Kerplunk*
14 **Westbound Sign -** *Insomniac*
15 **Walking Contradiction** - *Insomniac*
16 **Burnout** - *Dookie*
17 **The Panic Song** - *Insomniac*

> "Longview" is about masturbation!

> While Green Day was already a fairly big pop-punk band, the ballad "Good Riddance" skyrocketed them to

popularity. It's been said that Green Day wrote it in reaction to the disdain the underground punk scene felt toward the band once their 1994 album *Dookie* became popular.

> "American Idiot" comes from the Grammy-nominated album by the same title, which is a rock opera.

◀)) **If you like this, you might also like: the Ramones, the Clash, the Sex Pistols, blink-182, Sum 41, Good Charlotte.**

## GUIDED BY VOICES

01 **I Am a Scientist** - *Bee Thousand*
02 **Gold Star for Robot Boy** - *Bee Thousand*
03 **Motor Away** - *Alien Lanes*
04 **Game of Pricks** - *Alien Lanes*
05 **Don't Stop Now** - *King Shit and the Golden Boys*
06 **To Remake the Young Flyer** - *Under the Bushes Under the Stars*
07 **Big Boring Wedding** - *Under the Bushes Under the Stars*
08 **Choking Tara (Creamy Version)** - *Hardcore UFOs: Revelations, Epiphanies and Fast Food in the Western Hemisphere*
09 **Sad If I Lost It** - *Mag Earwhig!*
10 **Surgical Focus** - *Do the Collapse*
11 **The Brides Have Hit Glass** - *Isolation Drills*
12 **My Kind of Soldier** - *Earthquake Glue*
13 **Everywhere With Helicopter** - *Universal Truths and Cycles*
14 **Exit Flagger** - *Propeller*
15 **Chasing Heather Crazy** - *Isolation Drills*
16 **Girls of Wild Strawberries** - *Half Smiles of the Decomposed*

ESSENTIAL ARTISTS

17 **Echos Myron** - *Bee Thousand*

18 **A Salty Salute** - *Alien Lanes*

19 **Your Name Is Wild** - *Jellyfish Reflector*

20 **The Best of Jill Hives** - *Earthquake Glue*

21 **Learning To Hunt** - *Mag Earwhig!*

22 **Tractor Rape Chain** - *Bee Thousand*

23 **Not Behind the Fighter Jet** - *Mag Earwhig!*

24 **Lord of Overstock** - *Jellyfish Reflector*

25 **My Valuable Hunting Knife** - *Alien Lanes*

> Guided By Voices' lead singer, Robert Pollard, was a schoolteacher before he joined the band.

> Guided By Voices took the Strokes on tour with them . . . as an opener.

🔊 **If you like this, you might also like: Cheap Trick, Pavement, the Apples in Stereo, the Beatles, R.E.M., the Strokes.**

# GUNS N' ROSES

01 **It's So Easy** - *Appetite for Destruction*
02 **Live and Let Die** - *Use Your Illusion I*
03 **Mr. Brownstone** - *Appetite for Destruction*
04 **My Michelle** - *Appetite for Destruction*
05 **Nightrain** - *Appetite for Destruction*
06 **November Rain** - *Use Your Illusion I*
07 **One in a Million** - *G N' R Lies*
08 **Paradise City** - *Appetite for Destruction*
09 **Patience** - *G N' R Lies*
10 **Rocket Queen** - *Appetite for Destruction*
11 **Sweet Child O' Mine** - *Appetite for Destruction*
12 **Used to Love Her** - *G N' R Lies*
13 **Welcome to the Jungle** - *Appetite for Destruction*
14 **You Could Be Mine** - *Use Your Illusion II*
15 **Human Being** - *The Spaghetti Incident?*

**ESSENTIAL ARTISTS**

> Guns N' Roses lead guitarist Slash was born Saul Hudson on July 23, 1965.

> The band's singer, Axl Rose, was a choirboy as a kid.

> "One in a Million" contains incredibly offensive lyrics that are derogatory toward immigrants.

◀)) **If you like this, you might also like: Thin Lizzy, Hanoi Rocks, Cheap Trick, Mötley Crüe, Buckcherry, Great White.**

## BILLIE HOLIDAY

01 **When You're Smiling** - *The Quintessential Billie Holiday, Vol. 5: 1937–1938*

02 **A Fine Romance** - *Billie Holiday and Her Orchestra (1933–1937)*

03 **He's Funny That Way** - *Billie Holiday: The Legacy Box 1933–1958*

04 **I Cried for You** - *Billie Holiday: The Legacy Box 1933–1958*

05 **Billie's Blues** - *Billie Holiday and Her Orchestra (1933–1937)*

06 **Don't Explain** - *God Bless the Child*

07 **Easy Living** - *The Quintessential Billie Holiday, Vol. 4: 1937*

08 **Can't Help Lovin' Dat Man** - *The Quintessential Billie Holiday, Vol. 5: 1937–1938*

09 **Come Rain or Come Shine** - *Music for Torching: The Billie Holiday Story, Vol. 5*

10 **Foolin' Myself** - *Billie Holiday: The Legacy Box 1933–1958*

11 **God Bless the Child [Alternate Take]** -

Billie Holiday: The Legacy Box 1933–1958

12 **Lover Man [Live]** - Fine and Mellow

13 **The Man I Love** - Billie Holiday: The Legacy Box 1933–1958

14 **Me, Myself and I** - Billie Holiday and Her Orchestra (1933–1937)

15 **My Man** - Billie Holiday: The Legacy Box 1933–1958

16 **Good Morning Heartache** - The Essential Jazz Singers

17 **I've Got My Love to Keep Me Warm** - Billie Holiday and Her Orchestra (1933–1937)

18 **Strange Fruit** - Billie Holiday and Her Orchestra (1939–1940)

19 **Summertime** - Billie Holiday and Her Orchestra (1933–1937)

20 **Lady Sings The Blues** - Ultimate Jazz

21 **Night and Day [Alternate Take]** - Billie Holiday: The Legacy Box 1933–1958

22 **Solitude** - The Quintessential Billie Holiday, Vol. 9 (1940–1942)

23 **They Can't Take That Away from Me** - Billie Holiday and Her Orchestra (1933–1937)

24 **Trav'lin' Light** - Billie's Blues [Blue Note]

ESSENTIAL ARTISTS

> Billie Holiday was born Eleanora Fagan on April 7, 1915. Her mother was only thirteen at the time of her birth.

> U2 released "Angel of Harlem" in tribute to Holiday.

> Holiday's life was marred by drug and alcohol abuse; she died at the age of forty-four.

🔊 **If you like this, you might also like: Ella Fitzgerald, Frank Sinatra, Nina Simone, Sarah Vaughan.**

## MICHAEL JACKSON

01 **ABC** - *Michael Jackson & the Jackson 5*
02 **Bad** - *Bad*
03 **Beat It** - *Thriller*
04 **Billie Jean** - *Thriller*
05 **Black or White** - *Dangerous*
06 **Don't Stop 'Til You Get Enough** - *Off the Wall*
07 **Man in the Mirror** - *Bad*
08 **Never Can Say Goodbye** - *Anthology*
09 **P.Y.T. (Pretty Young Thing)** - *Thriller*
10 **Rock with You** - *Off the Wall*
11 **Scream** (duet with Janet Jackson) - *HIStory: Past, Present and Future, Book 1*
12 **Smooth Criminal** - *Bad*
13 **The Girl Is Mine** (duet with Paul McCartney) - *Thriller*
14 **The Way You Make Me Feel** - *Bad*
15 **Thriller** - *Thriller*
16 **Wanna Be Startin' Somethin'** - *Thriller*
17 **Somebody's Watching Me** - Rockwell album *Somebody's Watching Me*
18 **Blame It on the Boogie** - The Jacksons album *Destiny*

**ESSENTIAL ARTISTS**

19 **I'll Be There** - The Jackson 5 album *Maybe Tomorrow*

20 **Never Can Say Goodbye** - The Jackson 5 album *Maybe Tomorrow*

> Michael Jackson owns the bones of the Elephant Man and the Beatles catalog. Paul McCartney had given Jackson some friendly advice and told him that the real money in music was in publishing, so when the Beatles catalog was up for sale, Jackson outbid McCartney.

> One of Jackson's best friends is film legend Elizabeth Taylor.

> Jackson was once married and has three children, two of whom are named Prince Michael. (Incidentally, Michael's brother Jermaine has a son named Jermajesty.)

> Michael Jackson's distinct voice can be heard in Rockwell's "Somebody's Watching Me" (1984).

🔊 **If you like this, you might also like: Justin Timberlake, Usher, New Edition, \*NSYNC, Backstreet Boys, Prince.**

## THE JAM

01 **The Bitterest Pill (I Ever Had to Swallow) -** *Snap!*

02 **That's Entertainment** - *Sound Affects*

03 **Wasteland** - *Setting Sons*

04 **Carnation** - *The Gift*

05 **Thick as Theives** - *Setting Sons*

06 **Town Called Malice** - *The Gift*

07 **Down in the Tube Station at Midnight** - *All Mod Cons*

08 **Just Who Is the Five O'Clock Hero?** - *The Gift*

09 **English Rose** - *All Mod Cons*

10 **The Eton Rifles** - *Setting Sons*

11 **In the Crowd -** *All Mod Cons*

12 **Strange Town** - *Snap!*

13 **Pretty Green** - *Sound Affects*

14 **Beat Surrender** - *Snap!*

15 **In the City** - *In the City*

16 **Billy Hunt** - *All Mod Cons*

17 **Burning Sky** - *Setting Sons*

18 **Man in the Corner Shop** - *Sound Affects*

19 **"A" Bomb in Wardour Street** - *All Mod Cons*

20 **The Great Depression** - *Extras*

> This playlist was provided by Antony Ellis, lead singer of the Five O'Clock Heroes. His band is named after the Jam's "Just Who Is the Five O'Clock Hero?"

> The Jam's singer, Paul Weller, is known as "The Modfather."

> The Jam broke up in 1982.

🔊 **If you like this, you might also like: Buzzcocks, the Kinks, the Small Faces, the Clash, Elvis Costello, Joe Jackson, the Five O'Clock Heroes, the Ordinary Boys.**

ESSENTIAL ARTISTS

## JANE'S ADDICTION

01 **Jane Says** - *Nothing's Shocking*
02 **Been Caught Stealing** - *Ritual de lo Habitual*
03 **Mountain Song** - *Nothing's Shocking*
04 **Standing in the Shower . . . Thinking** - *Nothing's Shocking*
05 **Summertime Rolls** - *Nothing's Shocking*
06 **Ted, Just Admit It . . .** - *Nothing's Shocking*
07 **Stop** - *Ritual de lo Habitual*
08 **Idiots Rule** - *Nothing's Shocking*
09 **Classic Girl** - *Ritual de lo Habitual*
10 **Ain't No Right** - *Ritual de lo Habitual*
11 **Jane Says (live)** - *Kettle Whistle*
12 **Just Because** - *Strays*
13 **I Would for You** - *Jane's Addiction*

ESSENTIAL ARTISTS

> Jane's Addiction singer Perry Farrell went on to sing for the band Porno for Pyros. Guitarist Dave Navarro played guitar for the Red Hot Chili Peppers in the late nineties.

> Perry Farrell started the alternative music festival called Lollapalooza in 1991.

> Perry Farrell's DJ name is DJ Peretz.

🔊 **If you like this, you might also like: the Cult, Faith No More, Public Image Limited, the Music, the Flaming Lips.**

## ELTON JOHN

01 **Your Song** - *Elton John*
02 **Funeral for a Friend** - *Goodbye Yellow Brick Road*
03 **Someone Saved My Life Tonight** - *Captain Fantastic and the Brown Dirt Cowboy*
04 **Empty Garden (Hey Hey Johnny)** - *Jump Up*
05 **I'm Still Standing** - *Too Low for Zero*
06 **I Guess That's Why They Call It the Blues** - *Too Low For Zero*
07 **Sacrifice** - *Sleeping with the Past*
08 **This Train Don't Stop There Anymore** - *Songs from the West Coast*
09 **The Greatest Discovery** - *Elton John*
10 **Burn Down the Mission** - *Tumbleweed Connection*
11 **Friends** - *Friends*
12 **Tiny Dancer** - *Madman Across the Water*
13 **Rocket Man (I Think It's Going to Be a Long, Long Time)** - *Honky Château*
14 **Mona Lisas and Mad Hatters** - *Honky Château*
15 **Crocodile Rock** - *Don't Shoot Me I'm Only the Piano Player*

16 **Daniel** - *Don't Shoot Me I'm Only the Piano Player*

17 **Candle in the Wind** - *Goodbye Yellow Brick Road*

18 **Goodbye Yellow Brick Road** - *Goodbye Yellow Brick Road*

19 **Don't Let the Sun Go Down on Me** - *Caribou*

20 **I Feel Like a Bullet (in the Gun of Robert Ford)** - *Rock of the Westies*

21 **Tonight** - *Blue Moves*

22 **Song for Guy** - *A Single Man*

23 **Victim of Love** - *Victim of Love*

24 **Little Jeannie** - *21 at 33*

25 **Sad Songs (Say So Much)** - *Breaking Hearts*

26 **Nikita** - *Ice on Fire*

27 **I Don't Wanna Go on with You Like That** - *Reg Strikes Back*

28 **The One** - *The One*

29 **Circle of Life** - *The Lion King*

30 **Can You Feel the Love Tonight** - *The Lion King*

31 **Something About the Way You Look Tonight** - *The Big Picture*

32 **Original Sin** - *Songs from the West Coast*

> A British emo band named their band after "Funeral for a Friend."

> Elton John's performance at the 2001 Grammys with rapper Eminem garnered protests from the gay community, because of Eminem's often violent and homophobic lyrics.

> "Candle in the Wind," from *Goodbye Yellow Brick Road*, was not originally released as a single in the United States but it became a huge hit, most notably the version recorded following the death of John's friend Princess Diana of Wales in 1997.

> Bernie Taupin wrote the lyrics for most of Elton John's hits.

◀)) **If you like this, you might also like: George Michael, Scissor Sisters, Rod Stewart, Billy Joel.**

## JOY DIVISION

### JOY DIVISION

01 **Heart and Soul** - *Closer*

02 **Disorder** - *Unknown Pleasures*

03 **Isolation** - *Closer*

04 **Digital** - *Still*

05 **Transmission** - *Substance*

06 **Ice Age** - *Still*

07 **Novelty** - *Substance*

08 **Glass** - *Still*

09 **Atmosphere** - *Substance*

10 **Love Will Tear Us Apart** - *Substance*

11 **She's Lost Control** - *Substance*

### NEW ORDER

12 **Ceremony** - *Substance*

13 **Dreams Never End** - *Movement*

14 **Your Silent Face** - *Power, Corruption & Lies*

15 **Subculture** - *Low-Life*

16 **The Perfect Kiss** - *Low-Life*

17 **Blue Monday** - *Power, Corruption & Lies*

18 **Thieves Like Us** - *Substance*

19 **Temptation** - *Substance*

20 **Bizarre Love Triangle** - *Brotherhood*

21 **World in Motion** - *World in Motion*

22 **Fine Time** - *Technique*

23 **Regret** - *Republic*

24 **Crystal** - *Get Ready*

## ELECTRONIC

25 **Get the Message** - *Electronic*

26 **Getting Away With It** - *Electronic*

27 **Soviet** - *Electronic*

## REVENGE

28 **Pineapple Face** - *One True Passion*

## MONACO

29 **What Do You Want From Me?** - *Music for Pleasure*

30 **Shine** - *Music for Pleasure*

> This playlist includes songs from New Order, Electronic, Monaco, and Revenge, since all those bands emerged from Joy Division (after lead singer, Ian Curtis, hung himself in 1980).

> New Order immediately derived from Joy Division. Their first hit was "Blue Monday," which was more than seven minutes long.

> Electronic contained members of the Smiths as well as New Order.

◀◈) If you like this, you might also like: Interpol, the Killers, Pet Shop Boys, Erasure, Depeche Mode, the Faint.

## FELA KUTI

01 **Coffin for Head of State, Part 2** - *The Best Best of Fela Kuti*

02 **Water No Get Enemy** - *Expensive Shit/He Miss Road*

03 **Africa—Centre of the World** - *Afrobeat*

04 **Trouble Sleep Yanga Wake Am** - *Roforofo Fight/The Fela Singles*

05 **Original Sufferhead** - *Original Sufferhead*

06 **Zombie** - *Afrobeat*

07 **O.D.O.O.** - *Beasts of No Nation/O.D.O.O.*

08 **I.T.T., Part 2** - *Original Sufferhead/I.T.T.*

09 **No Agreement, Part 2** - *The Best Best of Fela Kuti*

10 **Yellow Fever** - *Yellow Fever/Na Poi*

11 **It's No Possible** - *Expensive Shit/He Miss Road*

12 **He Miss Road** - *Expensive Shit/He Miss Road*

13 **Pansa Pansa** - *Underground System*

14 **Sorrow Tears and Blood** - *Opposite People/Sorrow Tears and Blood*

15 **Shakara (Oloje)** - *Shakara/London Scene*

16 **Lady** - *Shakara/London Scene*

17 **Don't Worry About My Mouth O (African Message)** - *Stalemate/Fear Not for Man*

18 **Beasts of No Nation** - *Beasts of No Nation/O.D.O.O.*

19 **Teacher Don't Teach Me Nonsense** - *Teacher Don't Teach Me Nonsense*

20 **Upside Down** - *Upside Down/Music of Many Colours*

21 **Who Are You?** - *Buy Africa*

**ESSENTIAL ARTISTS**

> Fela Kuti is credited with inventing a style of music called Afro-Beat.

> Kuti died of complications from AIDS on August 3, 1997.

🔊 **If you like this, you might also like: Femi Kuti, Youssou N'Dour, Antibalas, Manu Dibango, Manu Chao, David Byrne (solo).**

## LED ZEPPELIN

ESSENTIAL ARTISTS

21 **D'yer Mak'er** - *Houses of the Holy*

22 **The Ocean** - *Houses of the Holy*

23 **Kashmir** - *Physical Graffiti*

24 **Down by the Seaside** - *Physical Graffiti*

25 **All My Love** - *In Through the Out Door*

> If you play the part of "Stairway to Heaven" that begins with "If there's a bustle..." until "...change the road you're on" backward, it sounds like Led Zeppelin singer Robert Plant is singing about Satan.

> All of Led Zeppelin's albums have reached the Billboard Top 10.

> There's a rumor going around that Robert Plant sold his soul to the devil in exchange for making Led Zeppelin the best rock 'n' roll band in history. Interestingly, one of Plant's influences was Robert Johnson, the original artist who sold his soul to the devil.

◀)) **If you like this, you might also like: the Rolling Stones, Alice in Chains, the White Stripes, Black Sabbath.**

ESSENTIAL ARTISTS

## MADONNA

01 **Borderline** - *Madonna*
02 **Everybody** - *Madonna*
03 **Express Yourself** - *Like a Prayer*
04 **Holiday** - *Madonna*
05 **Into the Groove** - *Like a Virgin*
06 **Like a Prayer** - *Like a Prayer*
07 **Like a Virgin** - *Like a Virgin*
08 **Material Girl** - *Like a Virgin*
09 **Open Your Heart** - *True Blue*
10 **Papa Don't Preach** - *True Blue*
11 **Ray of Light** - *Ray of Light*
12 **True Blue** - *True Blue*
13 **Vogue** - *The Immaculate Collection*
14 **Who's That Girl** - *Who's That Girl*
15 **Bedtime Story** - *Bedtime Stories*
16 **Burning Up** - *Madonna*
17 **Cherish** - *Like a Prayer*
18 **Deeper and Deeper** - *Erotica*
19 **Don't Tell Me** - *Music*
20 **Dress You Up** - *Like a Virgin*
21 **Live to Tell** - *True Blue*
22 **La Isla Bonita** - *True Blue*

23 **Lucky Star** - *Madonna*
24 **Oh Father** - *Like a Prayer*

> Not many people are aware of this, but "Bedtime Story" was actually written by Björk. This explains why it's really fucking good.

> Madonna was once married to film actor Sean Penn before she met husband Guy Ritchie.

> While not known for her acting skills, Madonna won a Golden Globe for her starring performance in *Evita*.

🔊 **If you like this, you might also like: Björk, Britney Spears, Cyndi Lauper, Kylie Minogue, George Michael, Janet Jackson.**

ESSENTIAL ARTISTS

## THE MAMAS & THE PAPAS

01 **California Dreamin'** - *If You Can Believe Your Eyes and Ears*
02 **Creeque Alley** - *Deliver*
03 **Dancing Bear** - *The Mamas and the Papas*
04 **Dedicated to the One I Love** - *Deliver*
05 **For the Love of Ivy** - *Papas & Mamas*
06 **Go Where You Wanna Go** - *If You Can Believe Your Eyes and Ears*
07 **I Call Your Name** - *If You Can Believe Your Eyes and Ears*
08 **I Saw Her Again** - *The Mamas and the Papas*
09 **Twist and Shout** - *Deliver*
10 **My Girl** - *Deliver*
11 **Somebody Groovy** - *If You Can Believe Your Eyes and Ears*
12 **Got a Feelin'** - *If You Can Believe Your Eyes and Ears*
13 **Look Through My Window** - *Deliver*
14 **Twelve-Thirty (Young Girls Are Coming to the Canyon)** - *Papas & Mamas*
15 **Straight Shooter** - *If You Can Believe Your Eyes and Ears*

16 **Monday, Monday** - *If You Can Believe Your Eyes and Ears*

17 **There She Goes** - Michelle Phillips solo album *Victim of Romance*

18 **Step Out** - *People Like Us*

19 **Dancing in the Street** - *The Mamas and the Papas*

20 **Dream a Little Dream of Me** - *Papas & Mamas*

> Michelle Phillips and John Phillips were married.

> John Phillips was previously in the Journeymen.

> By the time their second self-titled album was released, the Mamas & the Papas had replaced Michelle Phillips with Jill Gibson. Michelle had become involved with Denny Doherty and subsequently had an affair with Gene Clark of the Byrds, which caused tension in the band. But she soon returned.

◀)) **If you like this, you might also like: the Beach Boys, the Byrds, the Beatles, Simon & Garfunkel, the Turtles.**

# BOB MARLEY

01 **Lively Up Yourself** - *Natty Dread*
02 **Bend Down Low** - *Natty Dread*
03 **Put It On** - *Burnin'*
04 **Sun Is Shining** - *Kaya*
05 **Thank You Lord** - *Songs of Freedom*
06 **Guava Jelly** - *Songs of Freedom*
07 **Mellow Mood** - *Songs of Freedom*
08 **Stir It Up** - *Babylon by Bus*
09 **Kinky Reggae** - *Catch a Fire*
10 **Concrete Jungle** - *Catch a Fire*
11 **Simmer Down** - *Songs of Freedom*
12 **Caution** - *Songs of Freedom*
13 **Waiting in Vain** - *Dreams of Freedom*
14 **I'm Hurting Inside** - *Songs of Freedom*
15 **Burnin' and Lootin'** - *Burnin'*
16 **Who the Cap Fit** - *Rastaman Vibration*
17 **Jah Live** - *Rastaman Vibration*
18 **Hypocrites** - *Songs of Freedom*
19 **Iron, Lion, Zion** - *Songs of Freedom*
20 **Crazy Baldheads** - *Rastaman Vibration*
21 **Rat Race** - *Babylon by Bus*
22 **Get Up, Stand Up** - *Burnin'*

23 **War** - *Babylon By Bus*
24 **Running Away** - *Kaya*
25 **Redemption Song** - *Uprising*

> Bob Marley was once in a vocal group called the Teenagers with Peter Tosh, Bunny Livingston, Junior Braithwaite, Beverly Kelso, and Cherry Smith.

> Eric Clapton recorded Marley's "I Shot the Sheriff" in 1974 and it became a top ten hit.

🔊 **If you like this, you might also like: Peter Tosh, Bunny Wailer, Israel Vibration, the Pioneers, Ziggy Marley, Sublime, the Clash.**

## GEORGE MICHAEL

01 **Careless Whisper** - Wham! album *Make It Big*

02 **Don't Let the Sun Go Down on Me** - *Don't Let the Sun Go Down on Me*

03 **Faith** - *Faith*

04 **Father Figure** - *Faith*

05 **Freedom 90** - *Listen Without Prejudice, Vol. 1*

06 **I Want Your Sex, Pt. 1 & 2** - *Faith*

07 **Jesus to a Child** - *Older*

08 **Kissing a Fool** - *Faith*

09 **Monkey** - *Faith*

10 **Too Funky** - compilation album *Red Hot + Dance*

11 **Bad Boys** - Wham! album *Fantastic*

12 **Wake Me Up Before You Go-Go** - Wham! album *Make It Big*

13 **Last Christmas** - Wham! album *Music from the Edge of Heaven*

**ESSENTIAL ARTISTS**

> George Michael was born Yorgos Kyriacos Panayiotou on June 25, 1963, in north London.

> The first song George Michael ever wrote, at the age of seventeen, was "Careless Whisper" for Wham!'s 1984 album *Make It Big*.

🔊 **If you like this, you might also like: Robbie Williams, Scissor Sisters, Queen, Michael Jackson, Take That.**

## NINE INCH NAILS

01 **Perfect Drug** - soundtrack to *Lost Highway*
02 **Terrible Lie** - *Pretty Hate Machine*
03 **Hurt** - *The Downward Spiral*
04 **Where Is Everybody?** - *The Fragile*
05 **Wish** - *Broken*
06 **Into the Void** - *The Fragile*
07 **The Becoming** - *The Downward Spiral*
08 **Closer** - *The Downward Spiral*
09 **March of the Pigs** - *The Downward Spiral*
10 **Piggy** - *The Downward Spiral*
11 **Something I Can Never Have** - *Pretty Hate Machine*
12 **All the Love in the World** - *With Teeth*
13 **The Wretched** - *The Fragile*
14 **The Day the World Went Away** - *The Fragile*
15 **We're in This Together** - *The Fragile*
16 **Starfuckers Inc. (version 2)** - *Things Falling Apart*
17 **Every Day Is Exactly the Same** - *With Teeth*
18 **Dead Souls** - soundtrack to *The Crow*
19 **Burn** - soundtrack to *Natural Born Killers*
20 **I Do Not Want This**- *The Downward Spiral*

21 **Head Like a Hole** - *Pretty Hate Machine*

22 **Happiness in Slavery** - *Broken*

23 **Heresy** - *The Downward Spiral*

24 **La Mer** - *The Fragile*

25 **Getting Smaller** - *With Teeth*

26 **The Hand That Feeds** - *With Teeth*

> Singer Trent Reznor founded Nothing Records in 1992. He discovered Marilyn Manson and released Manson's first album on his label. Now former Marilyn Manson bassist Twiggy Ramirez plays in Nine Inch Nails. Also, former Icarus Line guitarist Aaron North plays guitar for the group.

> Former NIN member Richard Patrick now fronts the band Filter, which had hits with "Hey Man, Nice Shot" and "Take a Picture."

> Trent Reznor lived in New Orleans for ten years before moving to Los Angeles in late 2004.

🔊 **If you like this, you might also like: David Bowie, Marilyn Manson, KMFDM, Front 242, Filter, Skinny Puppy.**

**ESSENTIAL ARTISTS**

## NIRVANA

01 **Smells Like Teen Spirit** - *Nevermind*
02 **Serve the Servants** - *In Utero*
03 **Radio Friendly Unit Shifter** - *In Utero*
04 **Lithium** - *Nevermind*
05 **Pennyroyal Tea** - *In Utero*
06 **All Apologies** - *In Utero*
07 **Breed** - *Nevermind*
08 **Drain You** - *Nevermind*
09 **About a Girl** - *MTV Unplugged in New York*
10 **Aneurysm** - *Incesticide*
11 **Heart Shaped Box** - *In Utero*
12 **Rape Me** - *In Utero*
13 **Oh the Guilt** - *With the Lights Out*
14 **I Hate Myself and I Want to Die** - *With the Lights Out*
15 **Floyd the Barber** - *Bleach*
16 **Sliver** - *Incesticide*
17 **The Man Who Sold The World** - *MTV Unplugged in New York*
18 **Negative Creep** - *Bleach*
19 **Love Buzz** - *Bleach*
20 **Even In His Youth** - *With the Lights Out*
21 **Dumb** - *In Utero*

> Nirvana's original drummer was Chad Channing. He was replaced by Washington, DC, hardcore drummer Dave Grohl, who now fronts Foo Fighters.

> The band's lead singer, Kurt Cobain, was considered by many to be the voice of "Generation X." The weight of this title caused a lot of stress in Cobain's life, and combined with his addiction to heroin, may have been among the factors that led him to kill himself on April 6, 1994.

> Cobain was married to Hole's lead singer, Courtney Love, and together they had a daughter named Frances Bean Cobain.

> "The Man Who Sold the World" is a David Bowie cover.

🔊 **If you like this, you might also like: the Pixies, the Vines, early Silverchair, Hole.**

## NO DOUBT

01 **Just a Girl** - *Tragic Kingdom*
02 **Bathwater** - *Return of Saturn*
03 **Don't Speak** - *Tragic Kingdom*
04 **Ex-Girlfriend** - *Return of Saturn*
05 **Excuse Me Mr.** - *Tragic Kingdom*
06 **Sunday Morning** - *Tragic Kingdom*
07 **Hella Good** - *Rock Steady*
08 **New** - soundtrack to *Go*
09 **Simple Kind of Life** - *Return of Saturn*
10 **Spiderwebs** - *Tragic Kingdom*
11 **Trapped in a Box** - *No Doubt*
12 **Underneath It All** - *Rock Steady*
13 **Brand New Day** - *No Doubt*
14 **Magic's in the Makeup** - *Return of Saturn*
15 **Hey Baby** - *Rock Steady*
16 **Tragic Kingdom** - *Tragic Kingdom*

> Gwen Stefani is married to Bush singer Gavin Rossdale. They met while on tour in 1996.

> Eric Stefani, an original band member and brother of Gwen, left the band to become an animator for *The Simpsons*.

🔊 If you like this, you might also like: Save Ferris, the START, the Yeah Yeah Yeahs, the Specials.

## OASIS

01 **Live Forever** - *Definitely Maybe*

02 **Acquiesce** - *The Masterplan*

03 **Champagne Supernova** - *(What's the Story) Morning Glory?*

04 **Little James** - *Standing on the Shoulders of Giants*

05 **Cigarettes & Alcohol** - *Definitely Maybe*

06 **Don't Look Back in Anger** - *(What's the Story) Morning Glory?*

07 **Going Nowhere** - *The Masterplan*

08 **Born on a Different Cloud** - *Heathen Chemistry*

09 **Rock 'N' Roll Star** - *Definitely Maybe's the*

10 **Roll With It** - *(What Story) Morning Glory?*

11 **D'You Know What I Mean?** - *Be Here Now*

12 **Helter Skelter** - *Go Let it Out [EP]*

13 **Slide Away** - *Definitely Maybe*

14 **Some Might Say** - *(What's the Story) Morning Glory?*

15 **Stop Crying Your Heart Out** - *Heathen Chemistry*

16 **Supersonic** - *Definitely Maybe*

17 **Wonderwall** - *(What's the Story) Morning Glory?*

> "Little James" was the first album track to feature a song written only by Oasis singer, Liam Gallagher—all the earlier tracks were written by his brother, Noel.

> Moments before the band was set to perform acoustically for a taping of MTV's *Unplugged* series, Liam Gallagher pulled out. He said he was sick, but he spent the entire taping heckling his brother from offstage.

◀)) **If you like this, you might also like: the Beatles.**

## DOLLY PARTON

01 **9 to 5** - *9 to 5 and Odd Jobs*
02 **I Will Always Love You** - *Jolene*
03 **Islands in the Stream** (duet with Kenny Rogers) - *Greatest Hits*
04 **Jolene** - *Jolene*
05 **Here You Come Again** - *Here You Come Again*
06 **Baby I'm Burnin'** - *Heartbreaker*
07 **Love is Like a Butterfly** - *Love is Like a Butterfly*
08 **Two Doors Down** - *Here You Come Again*
09 **It's All Wrong, but It's All Right** - *Here You Come Again*
10 **Do I Ever Cross Your Mind** - *Heartbreak Express*
11 **Joshua** - *Joshua*
12 **Coat of Many Colors** - *Coat of Many Colors*
13 **My Tennessee Mountain Home** - *Love Is Like a Butterfly*
14 **Turn, Turn, Turn (To Everything There Is a Season)** - *The Great Pretender*
15 **Mama Say a Prayer** - *Love Is Like a Butterfly*
16 **D-I-V-O-R-C-E** - *In the Good Old Days (When Times Were Bad)*

ESSENTIAL ARTISTS

17 **Hold Me** - *Dolly: The Seeker/We Used To*

18 **More Where That Came From** - *Slow Dancing with the Moon*

19 **Why'd You Come in Here Lookin' Like That** - *White Limozeen*

> There is a theme park in Pigeon Forge, Tennessee, named Dollywood after Dolly Parton.

> Dolly Parton wrote the Whitney Houston smash hit "I Will Always Love You."

> The White Stripes covered Dolly Parton's "Jolene" in 2000.

> In addition to singing and songwriting, Parton has acted in a number of movies, among them *9 to 5* (1980) and *Steel Magnolias* (1989).

🔊 **If you like this, you might also like: Loretta Lynn, Kenny Rogers, Emmylou Harris, Patsy Cline.**

## PAVEMENT

ESSENTIAL ARTISTS

19 **In the Mouth a Desert** - *Slanted and Enchanted*

20 **Zürich Is Stained** - *Slanted and Enchanted*

21 **Here** - *Slanted and Enchanted*

22 **Stop Breathin** - *Crooked Rain, Crooked Rain*

> Pavement's final studio album, *Terror Twilight*, was produced by Nigel Godrich, who also produced Radiohead's *OK Computer*.

> Pavement's singer, Stephen Malkmus, is now in a group called the Jicks.

◀)) **If you like this, you might also like: the Pixies, Sebadoh, Guided By Voices, Yo La Tengo, Neutral Milk Hotel, R.E.M., Sonic Youth.**

ESSENTIAL ARTISTS

## PET SHOP BOYS

01 **Always on My Mind/In My House** -
   *Introspective*
02 **Closer to Heaven** - *Nightlife*
03 **Go West** - *Very*
04 **I Don't Know What You Want But I Can't
   Give It Any More** - *Nightlife*
05 **I Want a Lover** - *Please*
06 **It's a Sin** - *Actually*
07 **New York City Boy** - *Nightlife*
08 **Opportunities (Let's Make Lots of Money)** -
   *Please*
09 **Rent** - *Actually*
10 **Suburbia** - *Please*
11 **Time on My Hands** - *Disco 3*
12 **Tonight Is Forever** - *Please*
13 **West End Girls** - *Please*
14 **What Have I Done to Deserve This?** - *Actually*
15 **Why Don't We Live Together?** - *Please*
16 **You Only Tell Me You Love Me When You're
   Drunk** - *Nightlife*
17 **Two Divided by Zero** - *Please*
18 **Left to My Own Devices** - *Introspective*

ESSENTIAL ARTISTS

19 **Jealousy** - *Behaviour*
20 **Love Comes Quickly** - *Please*
21 **If Looks Could Kill** - *Disco 3*
22 **Being Boring** - *Behaviour*

> Pet Shop Boys vocalist Neil Tennant was a former editor at Marvel Comics, as well as a reporter for *Smash Hits* magazine.

> Tennant and keyboardist Chris Lowe chose the name Pet Shop Boys as a nod to friends who worked at a pet shop.

◀)) **If you like this, you might also like: Kraftwerk, New Order, Erasure, a-ha, Electronic, Depeche Mode, Alphaville, the Postal Service, Elkland.**

ESSENTIAL ARTISTS

## PINK FLOYD

01 **Another Brick in the Wall, Pt. 2** - *The Wall*

02 **Time** - *The Dark Side of the Moon*

03 **Comfortably Numb** - *The Wall*

04 **Money** - *The Dark Side of the Moon*

05 **Mother** - *The Wall*

06 **Nobody Home** - *The Wall*

07 **Us and Them** - *The Dark Side of the Moon*

08 **See Emily Play** - *Relics*

09 **Lucifer Sam** - *The Piper at the Gates of Dawn*

10 **Jugband Blues** - *A Saucerful of Secrets*

11 **Interstellar Overdrive** - *Relics*

12 **Careful With That Axe, Eugene** - *Relics*

13 **Young Lust** - *The Wall*

14 **One of these Days** - *Meddle*

15 **Have a Cigar** - *Wish You Were Here*

16 **Astronomy Domine** - *The Piper at the Gates of Dawn*

17 **Arnold Layne** - *Relics*

18 **Wish You Were Here** - *Wish You Were Here*

> The original Pink Floyd vocalist, Syd Barrett, had psychological problems and left the band in 1968. His song "Dark Globe" has been widely covered.

> Stoners discovered that Pink Floyd's *The Dark Side of the Moon* syncs up perfectly with the movie *The Wizard of Oz*. Here's how you do it:

> 1. Start the film.
>
> 2. When the MGM lion roars for the third time, press play on your music player.
>
> 3. Now get stoned. Do not get stoned before you do the above two steps or you'll probably mess up.

◀)) If you like this, you might also like: Radiohead's *OK Computer*, the Secret Machines, Peter Gabriel.

ESSENTIAL ARTISTS

## PIXIES

01 **Debaser** - *Doolittle*
02 **Here Comes Your Man** - *Doolittle*
03 **Allison** - *Bossanova*
04 **Velouria** - *Bossanova*
05 **Is She Weird** - *Bossanova*
06 **Where is My Mind?** - *Surfer Rosa*
07 **Hey** - *Doolittle*
08 **Monkey Gone to Heaven** - *Doolittle*
09 **Wave of Mutilation** - *Doolittle*
10 **Bone Machine** - *Surfer Rosa*
11 **River Euphrates** - *Surfer Rosa*
12 **Trompe le Monde** - *Trompe le Monde*
13 **U-Mass** - *Trompe le Monde*
14 **Winterlong** - *Dig for Fire*
15 **Manta Ray** - *Monkey Gone to Heaven*
16 **Into the White** - *Here Comes Your Man*
17 **Weird at My School** - *Monkey Gone to Heaven*

**ESSENTIAL ARTISTS**

> The band's original name was Pixies in Panoply.

> "Winterlong" is a Neil Young cover.

🔊 **If you like this, you might also like: Nirvana, stellastarr*, Placebo, Violent Femmes, Hole.**

213

## IGGY POP

01 **China Girl** - *The Idiot*
02 **Gimme Danger** - *Live at the Ritz NYC (1986)*
03 **I Wanna Be Your Dog** - *TV Eye (1977 Live)*
04 **Lust for Life** - *Lust for Life*
05 **Nightclubbing** - *The Idiot*
06 **No Fun** - *Live at the Channel (Boston, MA 1988)*
07 **Search 'N' Destroy** - *Sister Midnight*
08 **TV Eye** - *TV Eye (1977 Live)*
09 **Passenger** - *Lust for Life*
10 **Your Pretty Face Is Going to Hell** - *Zombie Birdhouse*
11 **Real Wild Child** - *Blah Blah Blah*
12 **Success** - *Lust for Life*
13 **Candy** - *Brick by Brick*
14 **Some Weird Sin** - *Lust for Life*
15 **1970** - *Live at the Channel (Boston, MA 1988)*
16 **Fun House** - The Stooges album *Fun House*
17 **Raw Power** - Iggy Pop & the Stooges album *Raw Power*

> Iggy Pop's given name is James Newell Osterberg, but he changed it when he founded the Stooges. At the group's concerts, he was known to roll around on broken glass on stage and dive into the audience.

> "China Girl" was not only cowritten and produced by David Bowie (as were many of Iggy Pop's early solo works), but it was also performed by Bowie in 1983 on his *Let's Dance* album.

◀)) **If you like this, you might also like: David Bowie, the Velvet Underground, the Doors, MC5, the Hives, the Icarus Line.**

ESSENTIAL ARTISTS

## ELVIS PRESLEY

18 **Jailhouse Rock** - *Jailhouse Rock*

19 **She's Not You** - *Pot Luck with Elvis*

20 **Too Much** - *Elvis*

21 **Treat Me Nice** - *Elvis' Golden Records*

22 **A Little Less Conversation (JXL Radio Edit Remix)** - *Elvis: 30 #1 Hits*

> "Always on My Mind" was also covered by the Pet Shop Boys.

> The 1861 ballad "Aura Lee" was the basis for the melody of "Love Me Tender."

> Elvis's first number one single was "Heartbreak Hotel."

> Elvis's twin brother, Jesse Garon Presley, was stillborn.

**ESSENTIAL ARTISTS**

🔊 **If you like this, you might also like: Roy Orbison, the Beach Boys, Fats Domino, Johnny Cash, Jerry Lee Lewis, El Vez.**

## PRINCE

01 **1999** - *1999*
02 **If I Was Your Girlfriend** - *Sign 'O' the Times*
03 **Delirious** - *1999*
04 **The Most Beautiful Girl in the World** - *The Gold Experience*
05 **Kiss** - *Parade*
06 **Let's Go Crazy** - *Purple Rain*
07 **Little Red Corvette** - *1999*
08 **Nothing Compares 2 U** - *One Nite Alone . . . Live!*
09 **Purple Rain** - *Purple Rain*
10 **Raspberry Beret** - *Around the World in a Day*
11 **Sign 'O' the Times** - *Sign 'O' the Times*
12 **Musicology** - *Musicology*
13 **For You** - *For You*
14 **Strange Relationship** - *Sign 'O' the Times*
15 **Darling Nikki** - *Purple Rain*
16 **Controversy** - *Controversy*
17 **Cinnamon Girl** - *Musicology*
18 **U Got the Look** - *Sign 'O' the Times*
19 **When Doves Cry** - *Purple Rain*

20 **Crazy You** - *For You*

21 **When U Were Mine** - *One Nite Alone . . .*
Live!

> Famously bald singer Sinéad O'Connor covered "Nothing Compares
  2 U" on her 1990 album, *I Do Not Want What I Haven't Got*.

> In 1993 Prince officially changed his name to an unpronounceable
  symbol and thus became known as the Artist Formerly Known as
  Prince. He changed it back in 2000.

> Prince was once involved with actress and model Carmen
  Electra.

🔊 **If you like this, you might also like: Chaka Khan, Rick
   James, Beck's *Midnite Vultures*, Outkast, Usher.**

**ESSENTIAL ARTISTS**

## QUEEN

01 **Bohemian Rhapsody** - *A Night at the Opera*
02 **Seven Seas of Rhye** - *Queen II*
03 **Killer Queen** - *Sheer Heart Attack*
04 **Flick of the Wrist** - *Sheer Heart Attack*
05 **Stone Cold Crazy** - *Sheer Heart Attack*
06 **Another One Bites the Dust** - *The Game*
07 **You're My Best Friend** - *A Night at the Opera*
08 **Love of My Life** - *A Night at the Opera*
09 **You Take My Breath Away** - *A Day At the Races*
10 **Somebody to Love** - *A Day At the Races*
11 **Good Old-Fashioned Lover Boy** - *A Day At the Races*
12 **Bicycle Race** - *Jazz*
13 **Don't Stop Me Now** - *Jazz*
14 **Play the Game** - *The Game*
15 **Under Pressure** - *Live Magic*
16 **Radio Ga Ga** - *The Works*
17 **I Want to Break Free** - *The Works*
18 **Is This the World We Created . . . ?** - *The Works*
19 **A Kind of Magic** - *A Kind of Magic*

20 **Who Wants to Live Forever?** - *A Kind of Magic*

21 **The Miracle** - *The Miracle*

22 **I Want It All** - *The Miracle*

23 **I'm Going Slightly Mad** - *Innuendo*

24 **These Are the Days of Our Lives** - *Innuendo*

25 **We Will Rock You** - *News of the World*

26 **We Are the Champions** - *News of the World*

> Queen's singer, Freddie Mercury, was born Farookh Bulsara in Zanzibar in 1946. He died in 1991 from complications from AIDS.

> The song "Bohemian Rhapsody" was prominently featured in the film *Wayne's World*.

> Queen's video for "Body Language" was banned by MTV for its racy nature.

**ESSENTIAL ARTISTS**

🔊 **If you like this, you might also like: Muse, Led Zeppelin, Gary Glitter, David Bowie, Liberace, My Chemical Romance.**

## RADIOHEAD

01 **Creep** - *Pablo Honey*
02 **Anyone Can Play Guitar** - *Pablo Honey*
03 **Pearly\*** - *Airbag/How Am I Driving?*
04 **The Trickster** - *My Iron Lung EP*
05 **Just** - *The Bends*
06 **Bones** - *The Bends*
07 **Street Spirit (Fade Out)** - *The Bends*
08 **Paranoid Android** - *OK Computer*
09 **High and Dry** - *The Bends*
10 **My Iron Lung** - *The Bends*
11 **Let Down** - *OK Computer*
12 **Airbag** - *OK Computer*
13 **Everything in Its Right Place** - *Kid A*
14 **Idioteque** - *Kid A*
15 **You and Whose Army?** - *Amnesiac*
16 **Like Spinning Plates** - *I Might Be Wrong: Live Recordings*
17 **There There** - *Hail to the Thief*
18 **Talk Show Host** - soundtrack to *Romeo + Juliet*
19 **True Love Waits** - *I Might Be Wrong: Live Recordings*
20 **Thinking About You** - *Pablo Honey*

> The band took its name from the members' least favorite Talking Heads song, "Radiohead Head."

> It has been said that the signature guitar cha-chunk sound in "Creep" was created by guitarist Johnny Greenwood as his way of protesting the song. He wasn't a fan of it.

> Most die-hard Radiohead fans view "Let Down," which was recorded in actress Jane Seymour's mansion, as the group's best song. However, the band rarely plays it live.

🔊 **If you like this, you might also like: Muse, Coldplay, Travis, JJ72, the Doves, Sigur Rós.**

**ESSENTIAL ARTISTS**

## RAMONES

01 **Rock 'n' Roll High School** - *End of the Century*
02 **The KKK Took My Baby Away** - *Pleasant Dreams*
03 **Gimme Gimme Shock Treatment** - *Leave Home*
04 **Sheena Is a Punk Rocker** - *Leave Home*
05 **I Wanna Be Sedated** - *Road to Ruin*
06 **Rockaway Beach** - *Rocket to Russia*
07 **Teenage Lobotomy** - *Rocket to Russia*
08 **Blitzkrieg Bop** - *The Ramones*
09 **Judy Is a Punk** - *The Ramones*
10 **Beat on the Brat** - *The Ramones*
11 **Cretin Hop** - *Rocket to Russia*
12 **I Wanna Be Your Boyfriend** - *The Ramones*
13 **Now I Wanna Sniff Some Glue** - *The Ramones*
14 **Pet Sematary** - *Brain Drain*
15 **Pinhead** - *Leave Home*
16 **She's the One** - *Road to Ruin*
17 **53rd and 3rd** - *The Ramones*
18 **Suzy Is a Headbanger** - *Leave Home*
19 **Too Tough to Die** - *Too Tough to Die*
20 **We're a Happy Family** - *Rocket to Russia*

> The Ramones were from Forest Hills in Queens, New York.

> The Ramones had originally recorded the song "Carbona Not Glue" for their album *Leave Home*, but it was removed because the company that made Carbona glue objected to its inclusion. It was replaced with "Sheena Is a Punk Rocker."

> None of the Ramones were related to one another.


🔊 **If you like this, you might also like: the Clash, the Sex Pistols, Blondie, the Beatles, Buzzcocks, Television.**

**ESSENTIAL ARTISTS**

## R.E.M.

01 **Bittersweet Me** - *New Adventures in Hi-Fi*
02 **Everybody Hurts** - *Automatic for the People*
03 **Fall on Me** - *Life's Rich Pageant*
04 **It's the End of the World as We Know It (and I Feel Fine)** - *Document*
05 **Losing My Religion** - *Out of Time*
06 **Man on the Moon** - *Automatic for the People*
07 **Near Wild Heaven** - *Out of Time*
08 **Radio Free Europe** - *Murmur*
09 **So. Central Rain** - *Reckoning*
10 **Talk About the Passion** - *Murmur*
11 **The One I Love** - *Document*
12 **At My Most Beautiful** - *Up*
13 **Bad Day** - *Bad Day*
14 **Crush with Eyeliner** - *Monster*
15 **Harborcoat** - *Reckoning*
16 **Dark Globe** - *Everybody Hurts*
17 **Daysleeper** - *Up*
18 **Imitation of Life** - *Reveal*
19 **Nightswimming** - *Automatic for the People*
20 **Shiny Happy People** - *Out of Time*
21 **What's the Frequency, Kenneth?** - *Monster*

> Kate Pierson from the B-52's sang on the hit "Shiny Happy People." She now runs a charming motel in the Catskills called Kate's Lazy Meadow Motel.

> R.E.M. has covered Interpol's "NYC" in concert.

> "Man in the Moon" was written about the comedian Andy Kaufman.

🔊 **If you like this, you might also like: Idlewild, Radiohead, the Smiths, the Pixies, the Talking Heads, Grant Lee Buffalo.**

ESSENTIAL ARTISTS

## THE ROLLING STONES

01 **(I Can't Get No) Satisfaction** - *Out of Our Heads*
02 **Brown Sugar** -*Sticky Fingers*
03 **Gimme Shelter** - *Let It Bleed*
04 **Honky Tonk Woman** - *Through the Past, Darkly*
05 **Jumpin' Jack Flash** - *Through the Past, Darkly*
06 **Let's Spend the Night Together** - *Between the Buttons*
07 **Paint It Black** - *Aftermath*
08 **Ruby Tuesday** - *Between the Buttons*
09 **She's a Rainbow** - *Their Satanic Majesties Request*
10 **Start Me Up** - *Tattoo You*
11 **Street Fighting Man** - *Beggars Banquet*
12 **Sympathy for the Devil** - *Beggars Banquet*
13 **Time Is on My Side** - *12 x 5*
14 **Wild Horses** - *Sticky Fingers*
15 **You Can't Always Get What You Want** - *Let It Bleed*
16 **Angie** - *Goats Head Soup*
17 **Rocks Off** - *Exile on Main St.*
18 **Tumbling Dice** - *Exile on Main St.*
19 **Torn and Frayed** - *Exile on Main St.*
20 **Happy** - *Exile on Main St.*

ESSENTIAL ARTISTS

> Before joining the Rolling Stones, Mick Jagger sang for Blues Incorporated.

> The Altamont concert in 1969 was an infamous one for the Stones because a fan was stabbed to death there by the Hell's Angels gang, who had been hired by the band to provide security at the show. The concert was documented in the film *Gimme Shelter*.

> The first Rolling Stones song to become an American Top 20 hit was "Time Is on My Side."

🔊 **If you like this, you might also like: the Beatles, the Who, the Kinks, the New York Dolls, the Hives, the Mooney Suzuki.**

ESSENTIAL ARTISTS

## SIMON & GARFUNKEL

01 **America** - *Bookends*
02 **Bridge Over Troubled Water** - *Bridge Over Troubled Water*
03 **I Am a Rock** - *Sounds of Silence*
04 **Mrs. Robinson** - *Bookends*
05 **Scarborough Fair/Canticle** - *Parsley, Sage, Rosemary and Thyme*
06 **The 59th Street Bridge Song (Feelin' Groovy)** - *Parsley, Sage, Rosemary and Thyme*
07 **The Only Living Boy in New York** - *Bridge Over Troubled Water*
08 **The Sound of Silence** - *Sounds of Silence*
09 **A Hazy Shade of Winter** - *Bookends*
10 **Cecilia** - *Bridge Over Troubled Water*
11 **Me and Julio Down by the Schoolyard** - *The Concert in Central Park*
12 **Wake Up Little Susie** - *The Concert in Central Park*

> "Mrs. Robinson" was originally called "Mrs. Roosevelt" after Eleanor Roosevelt.

🔊 **If you like this, you might also like: the Mamas & the Papas, James Taylor, Donovan, Cat Stevens.**

## FRANK SINATRA

01 **I've Got You Under My Skin** - *Songs for Swingin' Lovers!*
02 **I Get a Kick Out of You** - *Sinatra Sings Cole Porter*
03 **Summer Wind** - *Strangers in the Night*
04 **I've Got a Crush on You** - *Nice 'n' Easy*
05 **Night and Day** - *Sinatra and Sextet Live in Paris*
06 **Luck Be a Lady** - *Sinatra at the Sands*
07 **The Way You Look Tonight** - *I Only Have Eyes for You*
08 **Come Fly With Me** - *Come Fly With Me*
09 **Fly Me to the Moon** - *It Might As Well Be Swing*
10 **Someone to Watch Over Me** - *I Only Have Eyes for You*
11 **I Only Have Eyes For You** - *I Only Have Eyes for You*
12 **Everybody Loves Somebody** - *Portrait of Sinatra*
13 **Have Yourself a Merry Little Christmas** - *Christmas Songs by Sinatra*
14 **There's No Business Like Show Business** - *Portrait of Sinatra*
15 **Try a Little Tenderness** - *Nice 'n' Easy*

ESSENTIAL ARTISTS

16 **Blue Skies** - *Portrait of Sinatra*

17 **Embraceable You** - *Sinatra Sings Gershwin*

18 **The Lady Is a Tramp** - *Sinatra 80th: All the Best*

19 **You Make Me Feel So Young** - *Sinatra*

20 **They Can't Take That Away From Me** - *Songs For Young Lovers/Swing Easy!*

21 **Witchcraft** - *Sinatra 80th: All the Best*

22 **My Funny Valentine** - *Songs For Young Lovers/Swing Easy!*

23 **New York, New York** - *Sinatra: A Man and His Music With the Count Basie Orchestra*

> Frank Sinatra was born in Hoboken, New Jersey.

> His daughter, Nancy, was also a recording artist and together they recorded the song "Something Stupid," which was later covered by Robbie Williams and Nicole Kidman.

> Sinatra formed Reprise Records in the early 1960s.

> Sinatra had several nicknames, including "Chairman of the Board" and "Ol' Blue Eyes."

🔊 **If you like this, you might also like: Tony Bennett, Bing Crosby, Billie Holiday, Dean Martin, Sammy Davis Jr., Harry Connick Jr., Michael Buble, Jamie Cullum.**

ESSENTIAL ARTISTS

## SMASHING PUMPKINS

01 **1979** - *Mellon Collie and the Infinite Sadness*
02 **Bullet with Butterly Wings** - *Mellon Collie and the Infinite Sadness*
03 **Perfect** - *Adore*
04 **Pissant** - *Pisces Iscariot*
05 **Pug** - *Adore*
06 **Geek U.S.A.** - *Siamese Dream*
07 **Blew Away** - *Pisces Iscariot*
08 **Cherub Rock** - *Siamese Dream*
09 **Drown** - soundtrack to *Singles*
10 **The End is the Beginning is the End** - soundtrack to *Batman & Robin*
11 **Eye** - soundtrack to *Lost Highway*
12 **Frail and Bedazzled** - *Pisces Iscariot*
13 **Stand Inside Your Love** - *MACHINA/The Machines of God*
14 **Starla** - *Pisces Iscariot*
15 **Thru the Eyes of Ruby** - *Mellon Collie and the Infinite Sadness*
16 **Today** - *Siamese Dream*
17 **Tonight, Tonight** - *Mellon Collie and the Infinite Sadness*

ESSENTIAL ARTISTS

> "Blew Away" was written and produced by guitarist James Iha.

> "Today" was said to be Billy Corgan's suicide note. Fortunately, he never felt the need to use it—he's alive and well and living in L.A.

> "Landslide" is a Fleetwood Mac cover.

🔊 If you like this, you might also like: Muse, Kill Hannah, JJ72, James Iha's solo work, Placebo, the Cure, the Cars, Cheap Trick.

## ELLIOTT SMITH

01 **Waltz #2 (XO)** - *XO*
02 **Angeles** - *Either/Or*
03 **Baby Britain** - *XO*
04 **Needle in the Hay** - *Elliott Smith*
05 **Between the Bars** - *Either/Or*
06 **Bled White** - *XO*
07 **Clementine** - *Elliott Smith*
08 **Miss Misery** - soundtrack to *Good Will Hunting*
09 **Coming Up Roses** - *Elliott Smith*
10 **Independence Day** - *XO*
11 **Ballad of Big Nothing** - *Either/Or*
12 **Pitseleh** - *XO*
13 **No Name #1** - *Roman Candle*
14 **No Name #3** - *Roman Candle*
15 **Pictures of Me** - *Either/Or*
16 **Alameda** - *Either/Or*
17 **Punch and Judy** - *Either/Or*
18 **Roman Candle** - *Roman Candle*
19 **Son of Sam** - *Figure 8*
20 **Wouldn't Mama Be Proud?** - *Figure 8*
21 **No Name No. 5** - *Either/Or*

ESSENTIAL ARTISTS

> In 2003, after years of depression, Elliott Smith died from an allegedly self-inflicted sword wound.

> His song "Miss Misery," featured on the soundtrack to *Good Will Hunting*, earned him an Academy Award nomination.

> Smith was previously in the band Heatmiser.

◀) **If you like this, you might also like: Bright Eyes, Ben Lee, acoustic Nirvana, John Lennon.**

ESSENTIAL ARTISTS

## THE SMITHS

01 **Stretch Out and Wait** - *Louder Than Bombs*

02 **That Joke Isn't Funny Anymore** - *Meat Is Murder*

03 **Reel Around the Fountain** - *The Smiths*

04 **The Queen Is Dead (Take Me Back to Dear Old Blighty)** - *The Queen Is Dead*

05 **Accept Yourself** - *Hatful of Hallow*

06 **This Charming Man** - *The Smiths*

07 **Panic** - *Rank*

08 **The Boy with the Thorn in His Side** - *The Queen Is Dead*

09 **There Is a Light That Never Goes Out** - *The Queen Is Dead*

10 **Rubber Ring** - *Louder Than Bombs*

11 **Last Night I Dreamt That Somebody Loved Me** - *Strangeways, Here We Come*

12 **Still Ill** - *The Smiths*

13 **Heaven Knows I'm Miserable Now** - *Hatful of Hallow*

14 **Rusholme Ruffians** - *Meat Is Murder*

15 **This Night Has Opened My Eyes** - *Hatful of Hallow*

16 **Shoplifters of the World Unite** - *Louder Than Bombs*

17 **Unloveable** - *Louder Than Bombs*

ESSENTIAL ARTISTS

18 **Bigmouth Strikes Again** - *Rank*

19 **Please Please Please Let Me Get What I Want** - *Hatful of Hallow*

20 **The Headmaster Ritual** - *Meat Is Murder*

21 **Stop Me If You Think You've Heard This One Before** - *Strangeways, Here We Come*

22 **I Know It's Over** - *The Queen Is Dead*

23 **Some Girls Are Bigger Than Others** - *The Queen Is Dead*

24 **Sheila Take a Bow** - *Louder Than Bombs*

25 **How Soon Is Now?** - *Meat Is Murder*

ESSENTIAL ARTISTS

> This playlist was provided by Mark Spitz, whose novel *How Soon Is Never?* documents the efforts of Joe Green and his colleague Miki to reunite the Smiths. They are unsuccessful because Morrissey and guitarist Johnny Marr don't speak to each other.

> The lead singer for the Smiths, Morrissey, was born Steven Patrick Morrissey.

> Morrissey was a writer for the publication *NME* at one point.

> Drummer Mike Joyce and bassist Andy Rourke have toured together as DJs.

🔊 If you like this, you might also like: R.E.M., Radiohead, David Bowie, the Dears, Idlewild, the Cure, Interpol, the Killers, Suede, Pet Shop Boys.

## SONIC YOUTH

**ESSENTIAL ARTISTS**

19 **NYC Ghosts & Flowers** - *NYC Ghosts & Flowers*

20 **Rain On Tin** - *Murray Street*

21 **Tom Violence** - *EVOL*

22 **Schizophrenia** - *Sister*

23 **Dripping Dream** - *Sonic Nurse*

24 **Kool Thing**- *Goo*

25 **My Friend Goo** - *Goo*

> "Superstar" is a Carpenters cover and appears on a compilation album featuring other covers of the Carpenters.

> Sonic Youth members Kim Gordon and Thurston Moore are married and have a daughter named Coco.

> Thurston Moore is 6'6".

🔊 **If you like this, you might also like: the Velvet Underground, Television, the Stooges, Wire, Pavement, Meat Puppets, Nirvana, My Bloody Valentine.**

## STONE TEMPLE PILOTS

01 **Interstate Love Song** - *Purple*
02 **Art School Girl** - *Tiny Music . . . Songs from the Vatican Gift Shop*
03 **Big Bang Baby** - *Tiny Music . . . Songs from the Vatican Gift Shop*
04 **Creep** - *Core*
05 **Pop's Love Suicide** - *Tiny Music . . . Songs from the Vatican Gift Shop*
06 **Down** - *No. 4*
07 **Big Empty** - *Purple*
08 **Lady Picture Show** - *Tiny Music . . . Songs from the Vatican Gift Shop*
09 **Plush** - *Core*
10 **Pretty Penny** - *Purple*
11 **Sex Type Thing** - *Core*
12 **Church on Tuesday** - *No. 4*
13 **Vasoline** - *Purple*
14 **Wicked Garden** - *Core*
15 **Days of the Week** - *Shangri-La Dee Da*
16 **Glide** - *No. 4*
17 **I Got You** - *No. 4*
18 **Sour Girl** - *No. 4*

## 19 **Ride the Cliché** - *Tiny Music . . . Songs from the Vatican Gift Shop*

> Stone Temple Pilots singer Scott Weiland battled a heroin problem.

> Actress Sarah Michelle Gellar appeared in the video for "Sour Girl," which also featured Teletubbie-like characters.

> Scott Weiland now sings in the band Velvet Revolver with members of Guns N' Roses.

🔊 **If you like this, you might also like: early Pearl Jam, the Velvet Revolver, Soundgarden, David Bowie, solo Scott Weiland, Sponge, Bush.**

## BARBRA STREISAND

01 **A Star Is Born (Love Theme)** - *One Voice*

02 **Come Rain or Come Shine** - *Wet*

03 **Don't Rain on My Parade** - *Greatest Hits*

04 **God Bless the Child** - *Just for the Record*

05 **Happy Days Are Here Again** - *The Barbra Streisand Album*

06 **It Had to Be You** - *The Third Album*

07 **Memory** (Theme from *Cats*) - *Memories*

08 **Moon River** - *Just for the Record*

09 **My Favorite Things** - *A Christmas Album*

10 **My Funny Valentine** - *Simply Streisand*

11 **No More Tears (Enough Is Enough)** (duet with Donna Summer) - *Wet*

12 **Papa, Can You Hear Me?** - *Yentl*

13 **People** - *People*

14 **Send in the Clowns** - *The Broadway Album*

15 **Since I Fell for You** - *Barbra Joan Streisand*

16 **Someone to Watch Over Me** - *My Name Is Barbra*

17 **The Way We Were** - *The Way We Were*

18 **Tomorrow** - *Songbird*

19 **You Don't Bring Me Flowers** - *Songbird*

ESSENTIAL ARTISTS

> Barbra Streisand made her movie debut in the film *Funny Girl*, which won her an Oscar and a Golden Globe.

> Streisand is married to actor James Brolin.

🔊 **If you like this, you might also like: Bette Midler, Liza Minnelli, Cher.**

## TALKING HEADS

01 **Building On Fire** - *The Name of This Band Is Talking Heads*

02 **Psycho Killer** - *Talking Heads: 77*

03 **Mr. Jones** - *Naked*

04 **Once in a Lifetime** - *Remain in Light*

05 **Sugar on My Tongue** - *Popular Favorites 1976–1992: Sand in the Vaseline*

06 **Lifetime Piling Up** - *Popular Favorites 1976–1992: Sand in the Vaseline*

07 **Don't Worry About the Government** - *Talking Heads: 77*

08 **Warning Sign** - *More Songs About Buildings and Food*

09 **This Must Be the Place (Naive Melody)** - *Speaking in Tongues*

10 **And She Was** - *Little Creatures*

11 **Blind** - *Naked*

12 **I Wish You Wouldn't Say That** - *Popular Favorites 1976–1992: Sand in the Vaseline*

13 **Crosseyed and Painless** - *Remain in Light*

14 **Sax and Violins** - *Popular Favorites 1976–1992: Sand in the Vaseline*

15 **Life During Wartime** - *Fear of Music*

16 **Heaven** - *Fear of Music*

17 **Thank You for Sending Me an Angel** - *More Songs About Buildings and Food*

18 **Stay Up Late** - *Little Creatures*

19 **Television Man** - *Little Creatures*

20 **Take Me to the River** - *More Songs About Buildings and Food*

21 **With Our Love** - *More Songs About Buildings and Food*

22 **Houses in Motion** - *Remain in Light*

23 **Burning Down the House** - *Speaking in Tongues*

24 **Dream Operator** - *True Stories*

25 **I Zimbra** - *Fear of Music*

26 **Road to Nowhere** - *Little Creatures*

27 **Wild Wild Life** - *True Stories*

28 **(Nothing But) Flowers** - *Naked*

29 **Girlfriend Is Better** - *Speaking in Tongues*

> Singer David Byrne has a world-music-based record label called Luaka Bop.

> The Talking Heads came from the same NYC/CBGB's punk scene that spawned the Ramones and Blondie.

◀)) If you like this, you might also like: Arcade Fire, Franz Ferdinand, Radiohead, Television.

## U2

01 **Beautiful Day** - *All That You Can't Leave Behind*

02 **I Still Haven't Found What I'm Looking For** - *The Joshua Tree*

03 **I Will Follow** - *Boy*

04 **Mysterious Ways** - *Achtung Baby*

05 **Three Sunrises** - *Wide Awake In America*

06 **Love Comes Tumbling** - *Wide Awake In America*

07 **New Year's Day** - *War*

08 **One** - *Achtung Baby*

09 **Pride (In The Name of Love)** - *The Unforgettable Fire*

10 **Sunday Bloody Sunday** - *War*

11 **The Unforgettable Fire** - *The Unforgettable Fire*

12 **Vertigo** - *How To Dismantle an Atomic Bomb*

13 **Where the Streets Have No Name** - *The Joshua Tree*

14 **With or Without You** - *The Joshua Tree*

15 **Elevation** - *All That You Can't Leave Behind*

16 **Even Better Than the Real Thing** - *Achtung Baby*

ESSENTIAL ARTISTS

17 **Sweetest Thing** - *Where the Streets Have No Name*

18 **Two Hearts Beat as One** - *War*

19 **Walk On** - *All That You Can't Leave Behind*

20 **Another Time, Another Place** - *Boy*

21 **Running to Stand Still** - *The Joshua Tree*

22 **40** - *War*

**ESSENTIAL ARTISTS**

> The cover of *Joshua Tree* was actually shot in Arizona, not Joshua Tree National Park, California.

> Bono, The Edge, Larry Mullen, and Adam Clayton started out as "Feedback" before changing their name to "The Hype," and eventually settled on "U2."

> U2's singer Bono is well respected by politicians and is considered an expert in foreign debt. He has been considered for the Nobel Peace Prize for his efforts in erasing Third World debt.

> Bono was born Paul Hewson, and the Edge was born David Evans.

🔊 **If you like this, you might also like: Radiohead, Coldplay, the Alarm, R.E.M., INXS, the Stone Roses.**

# THE VELVET UNDERGROUND

01 **Heroin** - *The Velvet Underground & Nico*
02 **I'm Waiting for the Man** - *The Velvet Underground & Nico*
03 **Venus in Furs** - *The Velvet Underground & Nico*
04 **After Hours** - *The Velvet Underground*
05 **Beginning to See the Light** - *The Velvet Underground*
06 **European Son** - *The Velvet Underground & Nico*
07 **I Can't Stand It** - *VU*
08 **I'm Set Free** - *The Velvet Underground*
09 **All Tomorrow's Parties** - *The Velvet Underground & Nico*
10 **I'll Be Your Mirror** - *The Velvet Underground & Nico*
11 **Femme Fatale** - *The Velvet Underground & Nico*
12 **The Black Angel's Death Song** - *The Velvet Underground & Nico*
13 **Sunday Morning** - *The Velvet Underground & Nico*
14 **Pale Blue Eyes** - *The Velvet Underground*
15 **What Goes On** - *The Velvet Underground*
16 **Rock & Roll** - *Loaded*
17 **Sweet Jane** - *Loaded*

**ESSENTIAL ARTISTS**

18 **Jesus** - *The Velvet Underground*

19 **There She Goes Again** - *The Velvet Underground & Nico*

> The Velvet Underground was managed by pop artist Andy Warhol.

> Velvet Underground singer Nico was also a model and actress.

> Apparently, Lou Reed and Nico were involved in a relationship.

◀)) **If you like this, you might also like: Echo & the Bunnymen, Iggy Pop, Sonic Youth, R.E.M., Placebo, MC5, Joy Division, Nancy Sinatra, Primal Scream.**

ESSENTIAL ARTISTS

## WEEZER

01 **Undone—The Sweater Song** - *Weezer (Blue Album)*

02 **Burndt Jamb** - *Maladroit*

03 **December** - *Maladroit*

04 **Don't Let Go** - *Weezer (Green Album)*

05 **El Scorcho** - *Pinkerton*

06 **Getchoo** - *Pinkerton*

07 **Say it Ain't So** - *Weezer (Blue Album)*

08 **You Gave Your Love to Me Softly** - soundtrack
   to *Angus*

09 **Hash Pipe** - *Weezer (Green Album)*

10 **In the Garage** - *Weezer (Blue Album)*

11 **American Gigolo** - *Maladroit*

12 **Buddy Holly** - *Weezer (Blue Album)*

13 **Island in the Sun** - *Weezer (Green Album)*

14 **Jamie** - compilation album *DGC Rarities, Vol. 1*

15 **No One Else** - *Weezer (Blue Album)*

16 **Pink Triangle** - *Pinkerton*

17 **Slave** - *Maladroit*

18 **The Good Life** - *Pinkerton*

19 **The World Has Turned and Left Me Here** -
   *Weezer (Blue Album)*

20 **Tired of Sex** - *Pinkerton*

ESSENTIAL ARTISTS

> Weezer's lead singer, Rivers Cuomo, put the band on hiatus so he could attend Harvard University. The original Weezer bassist, Matt Sharp, is now the singer for the Rentals. Maya Rudolph from TV's *Saturday Night Live* was also in that band.

🔊 If you like this, you might also like: Buddy Holly, Cheap Trick, Nirvana, Death Cab for Cutie, Nada Surf.

# THE WHITE STRIPES

01 **Ball and Biscuit** - *Elephant*
02 **It's True That We Love One Another** - *Elephant*
03 **I Just Don't Know What to Do With Myself** - *Elephant*
04 **In the Cold, Cold Night** - *Elephant*
05 **Seven Nation Army** - *Elephant*
06 **The Hardest Button to Button** - *Elephant*
07 **There's No Home for You Here** - *Elephant*
08 **Jolene** - *Jolene*
09 **Sugar Never Tasted So Good** - *The White Stripes*
10 **Dead Leaves and the Dirty Ground** - *White Blood Cells*
11 **Fell in Love with a Girl** - *White Blood Cells*
12 **Hotel Yorba** - *White Blood Cells*
13 **I Think I Smell a Rat** - *White Blood Cells*
14 **We're Going to Be Friends** - *White Blood Cells*
15 **Let's Build a Home** - *De Stijl*
16 **Rated X** - *Hotel Yorba*
17 **You're Pretty Good Looking** - *De Stijl*

ESSENTIAL ARTISTS

> The White Stripes are known for wearing only three colors: red, black, and white.

> The White Stripes hail from Detroit, as do Eminem, Iggy Pop, and Madonna.

> Despite evidence that proves they were married, singer and guitarist Jack White still refers to drummer Meg White as his big sister.

◀) **If you like this, you might also like: Led Zeppelin, the Strokes, the Yeah Yeah Yeahs.**

## THE WHO

01 **The Kids Are Alright** - *The Who Sings My Generation*
02 **We're Not Gonna Take It** - *Tommy*
03 **My Generation** - *The Who Sings My Generation*
04 **Dogs** - *Rarities 1966–1972*
05 **The Seeker** - *Meaty Beaty Big and Bouncy*
06 **Bargain** - *Who's Next*
07 **Behind Blue Eyes** - *Who's Next*
08 **Won't Get Fooled Again** - *Who's Next*
09 **Baba O'Riley** - *Who's Next*
10 **My Wife** - *Who's Next*
11 **I Can See for Miles** - *The Who Sell Out*
12 **Long Live Rock** - *Odds & Sods*
13 **I Can't Explain** - *Live at Leeds (1995 Remaster)*
14 **Magic Bus** - *Magic Bus*
15 **Pictures of Lily** - *Magic Bus*
16 **Pinball Wizard** - *Tommy*
17 **So Sad About Us** - *A Quick One (Happy Jack)*
18 **The Real Me** - *Quadrophenia*
19 **Anyway, Anyhow, Anywhere** - *Meaty Beaty Big and Bouncy*
20 **Substitute** - *Who's Last*

> At the suggestion of the band's manager Kim Lambert, lead singer Roger Daltrey sang "My Generation" with a stutter to re-create the jitters of a speed addict.

> After original drummer Keith Moon's death, he was replaced by Kenney Jones.

> The songs "Bargain" and "Baba O'Riley" were used in car commercials.

◀)) **If you like this, you might also like: Supergrass, Nirvana, the Kinks, the Clash, the (International) Noise Conspiracy.**

ESSENTIAL ARTISTS

## >> CELEBRITY PLAYLISTS >>

## MENU

# >> CELEBRITY PLAYLISTS >>

The people in this chapter sing the songs you love, they play the songs you love, they remix the songs you love, they DJ the songs you love, they write about the songs you love, they write the books you love, and they quietly influence the bands you love through their Web sites. They could be you.

## DJ STEVE AOKI
### My Favorite Songs to DJ
**by Kid Millionaire**

01 **M.I.A.** - 10 Dollar
02 **Bloc Party** - Banquet
03 **LCD Soundsystem** - Losing My Edge
04 **Prince** - Kiss
05 **A Gun Called Tension** - Gold Fronts
06 **The Notorious B.I.G.** - Hypnotize
07 **Jay-Z** - I Just Wanna Love U (Give It 2 Me)
08 **Rick James** - Give It to Me Baby
09 **Mahjongg** - Hot Lava
10 **Bloc Party** - Price of Gasoline remixed by
   Automato
11 **2Pac** - California Love
12 **Michael Jackson** - Thriller
13 **Libretto** - Dirty Thangs
14 **DJ Kool** - Let Me Clear My Throat
15 **Jay-Z** - Public Service Announcement
   (Interlude)
16 **LCD Soundsystem** - Yr City's a Sucker
17 **Tom Tom Club** - Genius of Love
18 **The Spinto Band** - Oh Mandy

CELEBRITY
PLAYLISTS

19 **Amerie** - One Thing
20 **Snoop Dogg** - Drop It Like It's Hot
21 **Pharcyde** - Passing Me By
22 **Baldhead Slick** - I Win, U Lose
23 **M.I.A.** - Galang
24 **Phil Collins** - Easy Lover
25 **Rob Base & D.J. E-Z Rock** - It Takes Two
26 **Nu Shooz** - I Can't Wait

## THE CAESARS
### Current Playlist
**by Joakim Ahlund, guitarist**

01 **The Nerves** - Hanging on the Telephone
02 **The Left Banke** - Pretty Ballerina
03 **The Factory** - Path Through the Forest
04 **The Flamin' Groovies** - Shake Some Action
05 **Hüsker Dü** - Don't Want to Know if You Are Lonely
06 **Suicide** - Dream Baby Dream
07 **Bob Hund** - *Jag rear ut min själ*
08 **The Velvet Underground** - Sunday Morning
09 **Spacemen 3** - Hypnotized
10 **Electrelane** - The Valleys
11 **Karen Dalton** - Something on Your Mind
12 **The Only Ones** - Another Girl, Another Planet
13 **Sandy Denny** - Boxful of Treasure
14 **Yusef Lateef** - The Plum Blossom
15 **Tim Hardin** - If I Were a Carpenter
16 **Mazzy Star** - Fade Into You
17 **Brigitte Fontaine** - *J'ai 26 ans*
18 **The Rolling Stones** - Back Street Girl
19 **Roky Erickson** - Starry Eyes

20 **The Chills** - Pink Frost
21 **Guided By Voices** - Motor Away
22 **Johnny Copeland** - Ghetto Child
23 **The Rolling Stones** - Parachute Woman
24 **Stereo Total** - Holiday Innn
25 **Nico** - These Days
26 **Big Star** - Thirteen
27 **Bram Tchaikovsky** - Girl of My Dreams
28 **Buzzcocks** - Ever Fallen In Love?
29 **The Records** - Starry Eyes
30 **The Coral** - Pass It On
31 **The Creation** - Making Time
32 **Galaxie 500** - Strange
33 **Love** - Seven and Seven Is
34 **The Lyres** - Help You Ann
35 **Pram** - Cape St. Vincent
36 **Spacemen 3** - Come Down Softly to My Soul
37 **The Zombies** - Time of the Season
38 **White Noise** - Love Without Sound
39 **Ramones** - Outsider
40 **The Modern Lovers** - Roadrunner
41 **Linda Perhacs** - Chimacum Rain

## STEPHEN CHBOSKY
### Mix for the Triumphant Outcast

by the author of *The Perks of Being a Wallflower* and *Pieces*

01 **The Smiths** - Asleep
02 **The Beatles** - Dear Prudence
03 **Nick Drake** - Way to Blue
04 **The Magnetic Fields** - Parades Go By
05 **The Magnetic Fields** - The Book of Love
06 **The Kinks** - Young and Innocent Days
07 **The Replacements** - Skyway
08 **Tanita Tikaram** - Valentine Heart
09 **Cat Power** - Colors and the Kids
10 **Christina Aguilera** - Beautiful
11 **John Cameron Mitchell** - Wicked Little Town
   (from *Hedwig and the Angry Inch*)
12 **The Tragically Hip** - Ahead by a Century
13 **The Rolling Stones** - Moonlight Mile
14 **Simon and Garfunkel** - The Only Living Boy
   in New York
15 **Fleetwood Mac** - Landslide (Live)
16 **Amy Raasch** - Missing
17 **The White Stripes** - We're Going to be Friends

CELEBRITY

18 **The Shins** - Those to Come

19 **Doves** - Break Me Gently

20 **Peter Gabriel** - Wallflower*

21 **Nick Drake** - Fly (version from *Time of No Reply*)

22 **Sting** - Lullaby to an Anxious Child

23 **Jane's Addiction** - Summertime Rolls

24 **The Soundtrack of Our Lives** - The Flood

25 **Pearl Jam** - Elderly Woman Behind the Counter in a Small Town

26 **Coldplay** - Everything's Not Lost

> \*    Where I first heard the word "wallflower"

CELEBRITY

## DURAN DURAN

**Songs That Get Me Through the Day**

**by Simon LeBon, lead singer**

01 **Duran Duran** - Astronaut
02 **Young Disciples** - Apparently Nothing
03 **U-Roy** - Natty Rebel
04 **Johnny Clarke** - Declaration of Rights
05 **Iggy Pop** - Sixteen
06 **Iggy Pop** - Passenger
07 **Iggy Pop** - Funtime
08 **David Bowie** - Ashes to Ashes
09 **Donna Summer** - I Feel Love (12" version)
10 **Neil Young** - Heart of Gold
11 **Neil Young** - Old Man
12 **Mylo** - Destroy Rock & Roll
13 **2Pac featuring Dr. Dre** - California Love
14 **Underworld** - Born Slippy
15 **The Killers** - Somebody Told Me
16 **Joni Mitchell** - California
17 **Stan Getz and João Gilberto** - The Girl From Ipanema
18 **Bebel Gilberto** - *Samba e Amor*
19 **Nazare Pereira** - *Caixa de Sol*

CELEBRITY PLAYLISTS

20 **Sex Pistols** - Pretty Vacant
21 **The Damned** - Fan Club
22 **The Clash** - Rock the Casbah
23 **Franz Ferdinand** - Take Me Out
24 **Ludwig van Beethoven** - "Emperor" Concerto
25 **Dame Kiri Te Kanawa** - Faure's Requiem
26 **LCD Soundsystem** - Losing My Edge
27 **Lou Reed** - Walk on the Wild Side
28 **The Doors** - Riders on the Storm
29 **Elvis Presley** - Suspicious Minds
30 **Led Zeppelin** - Gallows Pole
31 **Jane Siberry** - The Lobby
32 **The Rolling Stones** - Street Fighting Man
33 **The Rolling Stones** - Tumbling Dice
34 **Oasis** - Cigarettes & Alcohol
35 **Joy Division** - She's Lost Control
36 **Duran Duran** - Still Breathing

## JENNY ELISCU

**A Mix for Your Mopey Ex-Boyfriend to Take with Him on His Band's Two-Month Tour, During Which, Long Drives Late at Night Should Afford Him the Opportunity to Think Long and Hard About How Much More Miserable He Is Without You**

by contributing writer Jenny Eliscu, *Rolling Stone*

01 **Wheat** - These Are Things
02 **Colin Hay** - I Just Don't Think I'll Ever Get Over You
03 **Matt Pond PA** - New Hampshire
04 **Wilco** - We're Just Friends
05 **Dashboard Confessional** - Living in Your Letters
06 **Bright Eyes** - You Will. You? Will. You? Will. You? Will.
07 **Built to Spill** - Fling
08 **Cat Power** - Good Woman
09 **Big Star** - Give Me Another Chance
10 **Seam** - Broken Bones
11 **Coldplay** - Warning Sign
12 **Death Cab for Cutie** - Title and Registration

CELEBRITY
PLAYLISTS

13 **Elliott Smith** - A Fond Farewell

14 **Leonard Cohen** - Hey, That's No Way to Say Goodbye

15 **Brand New** - The Boy Who Blocked His Own Shot

16 **The Sleepy Jackson** - Acid in My Heart

17 **Bob Dylan** - Don't Think Twice, It's All Right

18 **Sondre Lerche** - You Know So Well

## GOOD CHARLOTTE

**Songs to Listen to (Mostly by Morrissey) While Sitting in a Dark Hotel Room in London—Alone, Bored, and Uninspired . . .**

**by Joel Madden, lead singer**

01 **Morrissey** - Hairdresser on Fire
02 **The Faint** - How Could I Forget
03 **Morrissey** - Everyday Is Like Sunday
04 **Apoptygma Berzerk** - Kathy's Song (Come Lie Next to Me)
05 **The Smiths** - Heaven Knows I'm Miserable Now
06 **The Killers** - Everything Will Be Alright
07 **The Smiths** - There Is a Light That Never Goes Out
08 **Lou Reed** - Perfect Day
09 **Morrissey** - First of the Gang to Die
10 **Good Charlotte** - Ghost of You
11 **The Smiths** - Please Please Please Let Me Get What I Want
12 **Ben Folds** - Still Fighting It
13 **Morrissey** - Suedehead
14 **The Cure** - A Letter to Elise
15 **The Smiths** - The Boy with the Thorn in His Side

**CELEBRITY**

269

16 **The Flaming Lips** - Yoshimi Battles the Pink Robots Pt.1

17 **Morrissey** - Alma Matters

18 **HIM** - Pretending

19 **Good Charlotte** - The World Is Black

20 **Morrissey** - Now My Heart Is Full

**BONUS TRACKS JUST BECAUSE YOU ARE IN THE UK**

21 **Travis** - Why Does It Always Rain on Me?

22 **Oasis** - Cast No Shadow

23 **The Streets** - Stay Positive

24 **Muse** - Time Is Running Out

25 **Underworld** - Born Slippy

26 **David Bowie** - Modern Love

27 **The Clash** - Train in Vain

28 **Joy Division** - Love Will Tear Us Apart

29 **Depeche Mode** - Stripped

CELEBRITY PLAYLISTS

## THE ICARUS LINE

### Play Me

**by Joe Cardamone, lead singer**

01 **Captain Beefheart** - Lick My Decals Off, Baby
02 **James Chance and the Contortions** - Contort Yourself
03 **David Bowie** - Queen Bitch
04 **Funkadelic** - Can You Get To That
05 **Jesus and Mary Chain** - Teenage Lust
06 **John Lennon** - Cold Turkey
07 **Joy Divsion** - New Dawn Fades
08 **Kaleidoscope** - Dive Into Yesterday
09 **Lilys** - Will My Lord Be Gardening
10 **Love and Rockets** - Sweet Love Hangover
11 **Modern Lovers** - Government Center
12 **Os Mutantes** - *O Relógio*
13 **PIL** - Death Disco
14 **Primal Scream** - Some Velvet Morning (Two Lone Swordsmen Alt. Mix)
15 **Ride** - Tarantula
16 **Slowdive** - 40 Days
17 **Spiritualized** - Electric Mainline
18 **The Stone Roses** - Breaking Into Heaven
19 **Telex** - Moskow Diskow
20 **The Velvet Underground** - I Can't Stand It

## IDLEWILD

### The Last Twenty Songs I Listened To

**by Roddy Woomble, lead singer**

01 **Carl Perkins** - Everybody's Trying to Be My Baby
02 **Vashti Bunyan** - Winter Is Blue
03 **Crazy Horse** - Dance, Dance, Dance
04 **Baby Huey and the Babysitters** - Mama Get Yourself Together
05 **Bright Eyes** - Gold Mine Gutted
06 **Jerry Garcia** - Let It Rock
07 **Bonnie "Prince" Billy** - My Home Is the Sea
08 **Bob Dylan** - Visions of Johanna
09 **Martha Wainwright** - Bloody Mother Fucking Asshole
10 **Animal Collective** - Good Lovin Outside
11 **The Walkmen** - My Old Man
12 **Cat Power** - Cross Bones Style
13 **Neil Young** - Lookin' for a Love
14 **Ramones** - I Wanna Be Sedated
15 **Sandy Denny** - Milk and Honey
16 **Townes Van Zandt** - To Live Is to Fly
17 **AC/DC** - You Shook Me All Night Long
18 **Scott Walker** - Too Young to Know
19 **Jackson C. Frank** - Blues Run the Game
20 **Fred Blassie** - Pencil Neck Geek

## INTERPOL

### Twenty-five Tearjerkers

**by Carlos D, bass player**

01 **Sibelius** - Symphony No. 5, Second Movement
02 **Lefty Frizell** - Long Black Veil
03 **Joy Division** - Decades
04 **The Cure** - Plainsong
05 **Dead Can Dance** - Persephone (The Gathering of Flowers)
06 **Enya** - Watermark
07 **Beethoven** - Symphony No. 3, Second Movement
08 **Julee Cruise** - The World Spins
09 **Roy Orbison** - It's Over
10 **Glen Campbell** - By the Time I Get to Phoenix
11 **Cocteau Twins** - Cherry Coloured Funk (Seefeel Mix)
12 **Henryk Gorecki** - Symphony No. 3, First Movement
13 **Samuel Barber** - Adagio for Strings
14 **Albinoni** - Adagio
15 **Arvo Part** - Fratres
16 **Berlin** - Torture

17 **Clan of Xymox** - Medusa

18 **Pulp** - F.E.E.L.I.N.G. C.A.L.L.E.D.L.O.V.E

19 **Duran Duran** - The Chauffeur

20 **The Beatles** - Eleanor Rigby

21 **Black Sabbath** - Changes

22 **Book of Love** - Tubular Bells

23 **The Stone Roses** - I Wanna Be Adored

24 **Johnny Cash** - Hurt

25 **Led Zeppelin** - Since I've Been Loving You

## KAISER CHIEFS
### Top Ten Motown Tracks

10 **Edwin Starr** - Twenty-Five Miles

09 **Stevie Wonder** - Fingertips, Pt. 2

08 **Smokey Robinson and the Miracles** - The Tracks of My Tears

07 **Junior Walker and the All Stars** - (I'm a) Road Runner

06 **The Temptations** - I Can't Get Next to You

05 **The Isley Brothers** - This Old Heart of Mine (Is Weak for You)

04 **Martha and the Vandellas** - (Love Is Like a) Heat Wave

03 **Marvin Gaye and Kim Weston** - It Takes Two

02 **The Temptations** - Get Ready

01 **Stevie Wonder** - Uptight (Everything's Alright)

## KAISER CHIEFS
### Tour Bus Top Ten

10 **The Bar-Kays** - Soul Finger
09 **10cc** - Rubber Bullets
08 **Dexys Midnight Runners** - Geno
07 **The Beatles** - Everybody's Got Something to Hide Except for Me and My Monkey
06 **King Curtis** - Memphis Soul Stew
05 **Blur** - This Is a Low
04 **The Clash** - Train in Vain
03 **Elvis Costello and the Attractions** - (I Don't Want to Go to) Chelsea
02 **Queen** - Fat Bottomed Girls
01 **Glen Campbell** - Wichita Lineman

## THE KILLERS

### I Think My Spaceship Knows Which Way to Go*

**by Brandon Flowers, lead singer**

01 **Depeche Mode** - In Your Room
02 **The Commodores** - Nightshift
03 **David Bowie** - Drive-In Saturday
04 **Morrissey** - Trouble Loves Me
05 **Elton John** - Philadelphia Freedom
06 **John Lennon** - Gimme Some Truth
07 **U2** - Seconds
08 **The Cars** - Double Life
09 **Oasis** - Mucky Fingers
10 **Hall & Oates** - Rich Girl
11 **Elvis Presley** - It's Now or Never
12 **Jim Croce** - I Got a Name
13 **Oingo Boingo** - No One Lives Forever
14 **10cc** - I'm Not in Love
15 **XTC** - Making Plans for Nigel
16 **INXS** - Don't Change
17 **Bob Marley** - One Drop
18 **The Cure** - Six Different Ways

19 **The Beatles** - Let It Be
20 **The Killers** - All These Things That I've Done

* Lyric from David Bowie's "Space Oddity"

## THE KILLERS

### The Last Bunch of Songs I Listened to off the Top of My Head

**by Ronnie Vannucci, drummer**

01 **The Jimi Hendrix Experience** - Crosstown Traffic
02 **Tom Waits** - Jockey Full of Bourbon
03 **Talking Heads** - This Must Be the Place (Naive Melody)
04 **AC/DC** - Thunderstruck
05 **David Bowie** - Life on Mars?
06 **The Cure** - Push
07 **Johnny Cash** - Sam Hall
08 **Cake** - Mexico
09 **Blur** - Coffee & TV
10 **Led Zeppelin** - Rock and Roll
11 **Rocket From The Crypt** - On a Rope
12 **Fleetwood Mac** - You Make Loving Fun
13 **Warren G. and Nate Dogg** - Regulate
14 **Wilco** - Hell Is Chrome
15 **Morrissey** - Jack the Ripper
16 **The Beatles** - Because
17 **British Sea Power** - It Ended on an Oily Stage

18 **Tegan and Sara** - Take Me Anywhere

19 **Elvis Costello** - Radio Radio

20 **Lou Reed** - Vicious

21 **The Rolling Stones** - Ventilator Blues

22 **Elton John** - Goodbye Yellow Brick Road

23 **Ben Folds Five** - Selfless, Cold and Composed

24 **Steely Dan** - Dirty Work

25 **Pink Floyd** - Time

26 **Tom Petty and the Heartbreakers** - I Need
To Know

## CHUCK KLOSTERMAN

**The Most Frequently Played Songs on My iPod as Recorded by Technology as of January 19, 2005**

by the author of *Fargo Rock City*; *Sex, Drugs, and Cocoa Puffs*; and *Killing Yourself to Live*

01 **Albert Hammond** - It Never Rains in Southern California

02 **Amy Dalley** - Men Don't Change

03 **Barry Manilow** - Copacabana (At the Copa)

04 **Beastie Boys** - She's on It

05 **Belle & Sebastian** - I'm A Cuckoo

06 **Big Star** - Jesus Christ

07 **Black Oak Arkansas** - Hot and Nasty

08 **Bob Seger** - Hollywood Nights

09 **Body Count** - Cop Killer

10 **Bryan Adams** - Summer of '69

11 **Hear 'n Aid** - Stars

12 **Dolly Parton** - I Will Always Love You

13 **Donnie Iris** - Love Is Like a Rock

14 **The Doobie Brothers** - What A Fool Believes

15 **Eddie Rabbit** - I Love A Rainy Night

16 **Firehouse** - Don't Treat Me Bad

CELEBRITY PLAYLISTS

17 **George Strait** - All My Ex's Live in Texas
18 **Gretchen Wilson** - Redneck Woman
19 **Hanoi Rocks** - The Boulevard of Broken Dreams
20 **Jay-Z** - I Just Wanna Love U (Give It 2 Me)
21 **Jeff Beck** - Freeway Jam
22 **Juvenile** - Ha
23 **Kool Moe Dee** - How Ya Like Me Now
24 **Leon Redbone** - Come and Get Your Love
25 **Mariah Carey** - All I Want for Christmas Is You
26 **Maroon 5** - This Love
27 **The Move** - Brontosaurus
28 **Mu** - Paris Hilton
29 **Lindsey Buckingham** - Holiday Road
30 **Black Sabbath** - All Moving Parts (Stand Still)
31 **The Notorious B.I.G.** - Hypnotize
32 **Ozark Mountain Daredevils** - Jackie Blue
33 **Pat Benatar** - Precious Time
34 **The Walkmen** - The Rat

## MELODYNELSON.COM

### Playlist for the French and Those Who Love Them

**by Audrey Levy**

01 **Serge Gainsbourg** - *Requiem pour un con*
02 **Les Rita Mitsouko** - *Les histoires d'A.*
03 **M** - Close to Me
04 **Etienne Daho** - *Tombé pour la france*
05 **Lio** - *Le banana split*
06 **Plastic Bertrand** - *Ça plane pour moi*
07 **Téléphone** - *New York avec toi*
08 **Luna** - *La poupée qui fait non*
09 **Jacques Dutronc** - *Les cactus*
10 **Françoise Hardy** - *Comment te dire adieu?*
11 **France Gall** - *Poupée de cire, poupée de son*
12 **Brigitte Bardot** - Harley Davidson
13 **Carla Bruni** - *Le plus beau du quartier*
14 **Jane Birkin** - *Ballade de Johnny-Jane*
15 **Charles Aznavour** - *Le temps*
16 **Michel Berger** - *La groupie du pianiste*
17 **Vanessa Paradis** - *St. Germain*
18 **Yann Tiersen** - *L'absente*
19 **Jacques Brel** - *Ne me quitte pas*

20 **Françoiz Breut** - *Si tu disais*

21 **Serge Gainsbourg** - *La Javanaise*

22 **Keren Ann** - *Dimanche en hiver*

23 **Alain Souchon** - *Foule sentimentale*

24 **Charlotte and Serge Gainsbourg** - Lemon Incest

25 **Téléphone** - *Un autre monde*

## MIDTOWN

## Songs to Help Complete That 1 a.m. to 7 a.m. Van Drive While on Tour

### by Rob Hitt

Any touring band knows this drive, the one nobody wants to do. If only I was an enthusiast of a certain white drug then this drive would be easier. Being that I'm not, these are some of the songs that keep me alive when 4 a.m. rolls around and that morning dusk appears over the mountains while I am trying to make it in time for load-in at the next show.

### RED BULL #1

01 **Diana Ross** - I'm Coming Out
02 **Prince** - I Wanna Be Your Lover
03 **Carl Carlton** - She's A Bad Mama Jama
04 **The Cardigans** - Lovefool
05 **The Four Tops** - Same Old Song
06 **Gloria Jones** - Tainted Love
07 **Jackie Wilson** - Your Love Keeps Lifting Me Higher and Higher
08 **Meat Loaf** - Paradise by the Dashboard Light
09 **David Bowie** - Suffragette City

10 **Elvis Costello** - Radio, Radio

11 **Tom Petty & the Heartbreakers** - American Girl

12 **Iggy Pop & the Stooges** - Search and Destroy

13 **The Rolling Stones** - Under My Thumb

14 **Scandal** - The Warrior

15 **Midnight Oil** - Beds Are Burning

16 **Madness** - Our House

**RED BULL #1**

01 **Blondie** - Hanging on the Telephone

02 **Gang Of Four** - Damaged Goods

03 **The Human League** - Don't You Want Me

04 **Talking Heads** - Once in a Lifetime

05 **The Church** - Under The Milky Way

06 **Echo & the Bunnymen** - The Killing Moon

07 **The Sugarcubes** - 99 Red Balloons

08 **Depeche Mode** - People Are People

09 **The Specials** - Too Much Too Young

10 **The English Beat** - Tears of a Clown

11 **Fishbone** - Party at Ground Zero

12 **Mötley Crüe** - Kickstart My Heart

13 **Dinosaur Jr** - Start Choppin'

14 **Turbonegro** - The Age Of Pamparius

15 **At the Drive-In** - Heliotrope

16 **Q and Not U** - Soft Pyramids

## THE MISSHAPES

### Twenty-five Dance Floor Favorites

**by New York City DJ trio The MisShapes**

01 **Annie** - Heartbeat
02 **Franz Ferdinand** - Take Me Out [Daft Punk Remix]
03 **Pulp** - Mis-Shapes
04 **Madonna** - Burning Up
05 **New Order** - Blue Monday
06 **Mu** - Paris Hilton
07 **Le Tigre** - Deceptacon
08 **The Faint** - Worked Up So Sexual
09 **The Rapture** - House of Jealous Lovers
10 **Yeah Yeah Yeahs** - Y Control
11 **Siouxsie and the Banshees** - Cities in Dust
12 **The Smiths** - There Is a Light That Never Goes Out
13 **Bloc Party** - Banquet
14 **Gwen Stefani** - What You Waiting For?
15 **Interpol** - Evil
16 **Futureheads** - Hounds of Love
17 **Kate Bush** - Running Up That Hill
18 **Whitney Houston** - I Wanna Dance With Somebody (Who Loves Me)

CELEBRITY PLAYLISTS

287

19 **The Cure** - Boys Don't Cry

20 **Depeche Mode** - Personal Jesus

21 **Joy Division** - Disorder

22 **Sophia Lamar** - Rape Me*

23 **Nine Inch Nails** - Closer

24 **The Ronettes** - Be My Baby

25 **The Strokes** - Last Night

* This is a Nirvana cover.

CELEBRITY
PLAYLISTS

## THEMODERNAGE.ORG

**Twenty-five Songs to Play After Your Boyfriend Has Told You He Doesn't Love You (aka The Sad Bastard Mix)**

**by Laura Young (based on a true story)**

01 **Bettye Swann** - Don't You Ever Get Tired (Of Hurting Me)?

02 **Janis Joplin** - Piece of My Heart

03 **Bill Withers** - Ain't No Sunshine

04 **Marvin Gaye** - Ain't That Peculiar

05 **Heart** - What About Love

06 **Rufus Wainwright** - Foolish Love

07 **Morrissey** - The More You Ignore Me, the Closer I Get

08 **The Streets** - Dry Your Eyes

09 **Ryan Adams** - English Girls Approximately

10 **Bright Eyes** - Landlocked Blues

11 **Bob Dylan** - Just Like a Woman

12 **Harry Nilsson** - One

13 **Loretta Lynn** - Somebody Somewhere (Don't Know What He's Missin' Tonight)

14 **The White Stripes** - I Just Don't Know What to Do With Myself

CELEBRITY

15 **David Gray** - This Year's Love

16 **Travis** - Driftwood

17 **Beck** - Lost Cause

18 **The Shins** - Kissing the Lipless

19 **Snow Patrol** - On/Off

20 **Coldplay** - Trouble

21 **The Strokes** - Under Control

22 **The Bangles** - Eternal Flame

23 **Janet Jackson** - Again

24 **Blur** - To the End

25 **Stevie Wonder** - I Believe (When I Fall in Love
It Will Be Forever)

## DJ JUNIOR SANCHEZ

### My 35,000 Feet (Left Above the Clouds iPod Sound Check) Shuffle Mix

01 **Prince** - If I Was Your Girlfriend
02 **Peter Gabriel** - In Your Eyes
03 **Kate Bush** - Running Up That Hill
04 **The Smiths** - This Charming Man [François K edit]
05 **.38 Special** - Hold on Loosely
06 **Arcade Fire** - Rebellion (Lies)
07 **Babe Ruth** - The Mexican
08 **ESG** - Moody
09 **Benny Mardones** - Into the Night
10 **Berlin** - Masquerade
11 **Björk** - Joga
12 **Bikini Kill** - Strawberry Julius
13 **L7** - Pretend We're Dead
14 **The Breeders** - Cannonball
15 **The Buggles** - Video Killed the Radio Star
16 **Carly Simon** - You're So Vain
17 **The Cars** - Drive
18 **Cyndi Lauper** - She Bop
19 **Communiqué** - Perfect Weapon
20 **The Cover Girls** - Inside Outside

21 **The Cure** - Close to Me

22 **Kelis** - In Public

23 **Moving Units** - Anyone

24 **Philip Bailey and Phil Collins** - Easy Lover

25 **Depeche Mode** - I Want You Now

CELEBRITY

## SENSES FAIL
### Albums on My iPod
**by Buddy Nielsen, lead singer**

01 **Beck** - *Sea Change*
02 **Belle & Sebastian** - *The Boy With the Arab Strap*
03 **Born Heller** - *Born Heller*
04 **Calexico** - *Convict Pool*
05 **Christian Death** - *Only Theatre of Pain*
06 **Clinic** - *Winchester Cathedral*
07 **Depeche Mode** - *The Singles 81>85*
08 **Hot Snakes** - *Audit in Progress*
09 **Interpol** - *Antics*
10 **Kings of Convenience** - *Riot on an Empty Street*
11 **Ladytron** - *Light & Magic*
12 **Love and Rockets** - *Seventh Dream of Teenage Heaven*
13 **Medicine** - *Shot Forth Self Living*
14 **Morrissey** - *Viva Hate*
15 **Muse** - *Absolution*
16 **Phoenix** - *Alphabetical*
17 **The Cure** - *The Cure*
18 **The Distillers** - *Coral Fang*
19 **The Futureheads** - *The Futureheads*

**CELEBRITY PLAYLISTS**

20 **The Germs** - *(MIA) The Complete Anthology*
21 **The Honorary Title** - *Anything Else But the Truth*
22 **The Polyphonic Spree** - *Together We're Heavy*
23 **The Shins** - *Oh, Inverted World*
24 **The Streets** - *A Grand Don't Come for Free*
25 **This Mortal Coil** - *It'll End in Tears*
26 **Tones on Tail** - *Everything! (Disc 1)*
27 **Tones on Tail** - *Everything! (Disc 2)*
28 **Ween** - *Chocolate and Cheese*
29 **Weezer** - *Weezer (Blue Album)*
30 **Zero 7** - *When It Falls*

# SMASHING PUMPKINS
## Favorite Song Playlist
**by James Iha, guitarist**

01 **Big Star** - Thirteen
02 **Neil Young** - Birds
03 **Whiskeytown** - Avenues
04 **Gram Parsons** - $1,000 Wedding
05 **Elliot Smith** - Between the Bars
06 **Nellie McKay** - Really
07 **Tom Waits** - Martha
08 **Syd Barrett** - Terrapin
09 **David Bowie** - Drive-In Saturday
10 **Sly & the Family Stone** - Family Affair
11 **Willie Hutch** - I Choose You
12 **Barbara Mason** - Yes, I'm Ready
13 **The Friends of Distinction** - Going in Circles
14 **Prince** - I Wanna Be Your Lover
15 **Daft Punk** - Digital Love
16 **The Sounds** - Seven Days a Week
17 **Stars** - Ageless Beauty
18 **Fountains of Wayne** - Troubled Times
19 **Blonde Redhead** - Hated Because of Great
   Qualities

**CELEBRITY PLAYLISTS**

20 **Robbers on High Street** - Hudson Tubes

21 **Belle & Sebastian** - Women's Realm

22 **The Smiths** - Well I Wonder

23 **Joy Division** - Atmosphere

24 **My Bloody Valentine** - Lose My Breath

25 **The Velvet Underground** - After Hours

26 **Pixies** - Where Is My Mind?

27 **The Stooges** - T.V. Eye

28 **Slayer** - Angel of Death

29 **Eagles of Death Metal** - I Only Want You

30 **Van Halen** - Panama

31 **Journey** - Don't Stop Believin'

CELEBRITY
PLAYLISTS

## MARC SPITZ

**Highly Danceable New-Wave Songs I've DJ'd on Saturday Nights in New York City Bars in the Late Nineties That Inspired Bridge-and-Tunnel Weekenders and Acclaimed Actor Sam Rockwell\* to Angrily Request Something They Can Dance To . . . "Like Disco or Any Hip-Hop or James Brown or ABBA?"**

by the author of *How Soon Is Never?* and *We Got the Neutron Bomb*

01 **Mi-Sex** - Computer Games
02 **Human Sexual Response** - Jackie Onassis
03 **Sly Foxx** - Let's Go All the Way
04 **The Buggles** - Clean Clean
05 **The Godfathers** - Birth, School, Work, Death
06 **The Polecats** - Make a Circuit With Me
07 **Roman Holliday** - Stand By
08 **Donnie Iris** - Ah! Leah!
09 **Squeeze** - In Quintessence
10 **The Fabulous Poodles** - Think Pink
11 **Berlin** - The Metro
12 **Prince** - Jack U Off\*\*

CELEBRITY

13 **Big Audio Dynamite** - $E=MC^2$

14 **The Dominatrix** - The Dominatrix Sleeps Tonight

15 **Time Zone** - World Destruction

16 **Bronski Beat** - Why?

17 **Bauhaus** - Third Uncle

18 **Madonna** - Everybody***

19 **Tin Tin** - Kiss Me

20 **Hoodoo Gurus** - Like Wow—Wipeout!

21 **JoBoxers** - Just Got Lucky

22 **Madness** - Baggy Trousers

23 **The Belle Stars** - Sign of the Times

24 **Plastic Bertrand** - *Ça plane pour moi*

**BONUS LIST: NEW-WAVE SONGS ALL THE ABOVEMENTIONED BRIDGE-AND-TUNNELERS WILL ABSOLUTELY ALWAYS DANCE TO, AKA THE COMPROMISE JAMS**

25 **Duran Duran** - Rio

26 **Soft Cell** - Tainted Love (extended mix preferable)

27 **Yaz** - Situation

---

\*     Actually really nice. Really wants to hear James Brown. Will tip.

\*\*     Sometimes they do not know this is Prince.

\*\*\*     Sometimes they do not know this is Madonna.

## STEREOGUM.COM

### Before They Were Rap Songs

#### by Scott Lapatine

Once-cheesy tunes that found a new life in hip-hop. The rap song that samples each is listed in parentheses after the song.

01 **Tom Brock** - There's Nothing in This World That Can Stop Me From Loving You (Jay-Z - Girls, Girls, Girls)

02 **Brenda Russell** - A Little Bit of Love (Big Pun - Still Not a Player)

03 **Kool & The Gang** - Summer Madness (DJ Jazzy Jeff and the Fresh Prince - Summertime)

04 **Kenny Rogers and Dolly Parton** - Islands in the Stream (Pras - Ghetto Supastar)

05 **Bob James** - Mardi Gras (Run-D.M.C. - Peter Piper)

06 **George Clinton** - Atomic Dog (Snoop Doggy Dogg and Lil' Bow Wow - Bow Wow (That's My Name))

07 **DeBarge** - A Dream (2Pac - I Ain't Mad at Cha)

08 **Curtis Mayfield** - Superfly (Beastie Boys - Egg Man)

09 **Funkadelic** - (Not Just) Knee Deep (De La Soul - Me, Myself And I)

CELEBRITY

10 **Martika** - Toy Soldiers (Eminem - Like Toy Soldiers)

11 **Galt MacDermot** - Space (Busta Rhymes - Woo Ha! Got You All in Check)

12 **Stevie Wonder** - Pastime Paradise (Coolio - Gangsta's Paradise)

13 **Joe Simon** - Before the Night Is Over (Outkast - So Fresh, So Clean)

14 **Michael McDonald** - I Keep Forgettin' (Warren G. and Nate Dogg - Regulate)

15 **Grace Jones** - My Jamaican Guy (LL Cool J - Doin' It)

16 **Chic** - Good Times (The Sugarhill Gang - Rapper's Delight)

17 **The Delfonics** - Ready or Not Here I Come (Can't Hide from Love) (The Fugees - Ready or Not)

18 **Diana Ross** - I'm Coming Out (The Notorious B.I.G. - Mo Money Mo Problems)

19 **Freddie Scott** - (You) Got What I Need (Biz Markie - Just a Friend)

20 **Bernard Wright** - Spinnin' (Skee-Lo - I Wish)

21 **Roberta Flack and Donny Hathaway** - Be Real Black For Me (Scarface - On My Block)

22 **Charles Wright & the Watts 103rd Street Rhythm Band** - Express Yourself (N.W.A. - Express Yourself)

23 **Bruce Hornsby** - The Way It Is (2Pac - Changes)

24 **Lyn Collins** - Think (About It) (Rob Base & DJ EZ Rock - It Takes Two)

25 **Rick James** - Super Freak (MC Hammer - U Can't Touch This)

## TAKING BACK SUNDAY
### The Last Twenty Songs I Listened To
**by Matt Rubano, bass player**

01 **Björk** - Unravel
02 **Jeff Buckley** - Corpus Christi Carol
03 **Queens of the Stone Age** - In the Fade
04 **The Flamingos** - I Only Have Eyes for You
05 **The Mars Volta** - Miranda That Ghost Just Isn't Holy Anymore
06 **Cassandra Wilson** - Harvest Moon
07 **Shudder to Think** - X-French Tee Shirt
08 **Miles Davis** - Blue in Green
09 **Red Hot Chili Peppers** - Pea
10 **Fugazi** - Merchandise
11 **A Tribe Called Quest** - Award Tour
12 **Squarepusher** - A Journey to Reedham
13 **Squarepusher** - Come on My Selector
14 **Recover** - Night of the Creeps
15 **Ryan Adams** - Wonderwall
16 **Dub Trio** - Drive by Dub
17 **The Police** - Walking on the Moon
18 **Herbie Hancock** - Maiden Voyage (Live)
19 **Herbie Hancock** - Actual Proof
20 **Frank Sinatra** - New York, New York

## MENU

# >> OTHER PLAYLISTS >>

Sometimes it's those random moments in your life that are most in need of a soundtrack. Whether it's waking up in the morning, cleaning your house, or DJing a wedding, everything is better when there's a dynamic mix to keep the rhythm of things going, or not going, depending on the activity.

## ALTERNATIVE HAPPY-BIRTHDAY SONGS

Singing "Happy Birthday" is such a common thing to do on someone's birthday. Why not spice it up with something different? This would make a great mix CD to give someone on their special day.

01 **Pearl Jam** - Happy Birthday (from 04/05/03: North America - #18 San Antonio)
02 **Bright Eyes** - Happy Birthday to Me (Feb. 15)
03 **Joan Jett and the Blackhearts** - Too Bad on Your Birthday
04 **The Smiths** - Unhappy Birthday
05 **The Birthday Party** - Happy Birthday
06 **The Fall** - Birthday
07 **Altered Images** - Happy Birthday
08 **The Sugarcubes** - Birthday
09 **New Kids on the Block** - Happy Birthday
10 **Pet Shop Boys** - Birthday Boy

**OTHER PLAYLISTS**

## BABY BABY BABY—SONGS FOR YOUR BABY

You know how couples like to call each other baby instead of their real names? Wait, you're one of those couples? Yo, this playlist has your lover's name written all over it!

01 **Aretha Franklin** - Baby I Love You
02 **The Beatles** - Baby You're a Rich Man
03 **Belle & Sebastian** - Step Into My Office, Baby
04 **Blondie** - Pretty Baby
05 **Bow Wow Wow** - Baby, Oh No
06 **Cat Power** - Babydoll
07 **The Cure** - The Baby Screams
08 **Eddie Money** - Baby Hold On
09 **Graham Coxon** - Baby, You're Out of My Mind
10 **Head Automatica** - Beating Heart Baby
11 **Mazzy Star** - She's My Baby
12 **Metric** - Combat Baby
13 **Michael Jackson** - Baby Be Mine
14 **Muse** - Plug In Baby
15 **N.E.R.D.** - Baby Doll
16 **No Doubt** - Hey Baby
17 **Ol' Dirty Bastard** - [Baby I] Got Your Money
18 **Patsy Cline** - Back in Baby's Arms

OTHER
PLAYLISTS

19 **Queens of the Stone Age** - You Can't Quit Me Baby

20 **The Rolling Stones** - Have You Seen Your Mother Baby, Standing in the Shadow?

21 **The Ronettes** - Be My Baby

22 **The Smiths** - You Just Haven't Earned It Yet, Baby

23 **Spiritualized** - Oh Baby

24 **Stone Temple Pilots** - Big Bang Baby

25 **Britney Spears** - Baby One More Time

26 **Vanilla Ice** - Ice Ice Baby

27 **The White Stripes** - The Big Three Killed My Baby

OTHER
PLAYLISTS

## BACK TO SCHOOL

No matter how great the teachers are, how cool the school is, or how popular you are, going back to school can be a total drag. This is perfect for that yellow-bus ride in the morning, and definitely in the afternoon when you can't wait to get home.

01 **Deftones** - Back to School (Mini Maggit)
02 **Nirvana** - School
03 **Ramones** - Rock 'n' Roll High School
04 **Mötley Crüe** - Smokin' in the Boys' Room
05 **Pink Floyd** - Another Brick in the Wall, Pt. 2
06 **Van Halen** - Hot for Teacher
07 **The Police** - Don't Stand So Close to Me
08 **blink-182** - Going Away to College
09 **Alice Cooper** - School's Out
10 **Air** - Highschool Lover
11 **The Darkness** - Friday Night
12 **Kanye West** - School Spirit
13 **Langley Schools Music Project** - God Only Knows
14 **The Runaways** - School Days
15 **Stevie Nicks** - Edge of Seventeen
16 **The Who** - Substitute

17 **Stone Temple Pilots** - Art School Girl

18 **Chuck Berry** - School Days

19 **Doris Day** - Teacher's Pet

20 **Louis XIV** - Hey Teacher

## BAR MITZVAH JAMS

Kids celebrating bar mitzvahs don't really *know* music yet. They just want to dance with the girl or guy they like for the first time in a non-threatening setting. So mix it up. Play songs they'll know, the cheesy stuff, and things you think they should like.

01 **Neil Diamond** - Havah Nagila
02 **95 South** - Whoot, There It Is
03 **a-ha** - Take On Me
04 **69 Boyz** - Tootsee Roll
05 **Franz Ferdinand** - Take Me Out
06 **Kelly Clarkson** - Since U Been Gone
07 **Outkast** - Hey Ya!
08 **Gwen Stefani** - What You Waiting For?
09 **Coolio** - Fantastic Voyage
10 **Black Eyed Peas** - Let's Get it Started
11 **Britney Spears** - Baby One More Time
12 **Destiny's Child** - Jumpin Jumpin
13 **Keane** - Somewhere Only We Know
14 **Sir Mix-a-Lot** - Baby Got Back
15 **Danger Mouse** - 99 Problems
16 **Jennifer Lopez** - I'm Real

17 **Lipps Inc.** - Funkytown
18 **Electric Six** - Danger! High Voltage
19 **Beyoncé** - Crazy in Love
20 **C+C Music Factory** - Gonna Make You Sweat
    (Everybody Dance Now)
21 **Dionne Warwick** - That's What Friends Are For
22 **Jet** - Are You Gonna Be My Girl

OTHER
PLAYLISTS

## CAR SEX SONGS

Practice safe sex and safe driving, but never at the same time!

01 **Black Rebel Motorcycle Club** - Love Burns
02 **Arcade Fire** - In the Backseat
03 **Scissor Sisters** - Lovers in the Backseat
04 **Bobby Womack** - Across 110th Street
05 **Brian Wilson** - Good Vibrations
06 **Frank Sinatra** - Strangers in the Night
07 **The Beatles** - Drive My Car
08 **The Killers** - Midnight Show
09 **Blur** - M.O.R.
10 **The B-52's** - Roam
11 **Björk** - Big Time Sensuality
12 **The Teeth** - Peter Goes To 43rd Street
13 **Air** - Sexy Boy
14 **D'Angelo** - Untitled (How Does It Feel?)
15 **Curtis Mayfield** - Superfly
16 **Elastica** - Car Song
17 **The Chemical Brothers** - Out of Control
18 **The Beatles** - Ticket to Ride

## CAR SING-ALONG SONGS

You know those scenes in movies when everyone's in a car or a bus and then there's a song playing on the stereo and everyone breaks away from their zoning off and starts singing along, creating this beautiful unforgettable moment? Well, here is a mix for an extended ride in a vehicle packed with people who need to bond by singing along to the same song. Eat your heart out, Cameron Crowe.

01 **Queen** - Bohemian Rhapsody
02 **Billy Joel** - Piano Man
03 **The Rolling Stones** - Wild Horses
04 **Elton John** - Tiny Dancer
05 **Coldplay** - Yellow
06 **Kelly Clarkson** - Since U Been Gone
07 **Neil Diamond** - Sweet Caroline
08 **Led Zeppelin** - Immigrant Song
09 **The Black Crowes** - Hard to Handle
10 **The Beatles** - Hey Jude
11 **Violent Femmes** - Blister in the Sun
12 **Pulp** - Common People
13 **Queen** (featuring David Bowie) - Under Pressure
14 **David Bowie** - Suffragette City

**OTHER PLAYLISTS**

15 **Oasis** - Wonderwall
16 **Pearl Jam** - Alive
17 **The Smiths** - Panic
18 **Bonnie Tyler** - Total Eclipse of the Heart
19 **Pixies** - Where Is My Mind?
20 **The Commodores** - Easy
21 **Social Distortion** - Story of My Life
22 **The Clash** - Should I Stay or Should I Go
23 **Counting Crows** - Mr. Jones
24 **James** - Laid
25 **A Tribe Called Quest** - Scenario
26 **Ace of Base** - The Sign
27 **Elvis Costello** - Alison

## DRUGS DO WORK

I'm not condoning drug use. Drugs are bad. But some songs are about drugs—about how they're bad or how they're good. Here are some of them. For legal reasons, I'm urging you to not find out why drugs are bad or good.

01 **The Dandy Warhols** - Not If You Were The Last Junkie On Earth
02 **The Brian Jonestown Massacre** - Wasted
03 **Mazzy Star** - Wasted
04 **Action Action** - Drug Like
05 **Giant Drag** - Drugs
06 **The Beatles** - Yellow Submarine*
07 **Buckcherry** - Lit Up
08 **Sonic Youth** - I Love You Mary Jane
09 **Cypress Hill** - Hits From The Bong
10 **Manic Street Preachers** - Drug Drug Druggy
11 **The Cure** - Numb
12 **Afroman** - Because I Got High
13 **Rancid** - Dope Sick Girl
14 **The Offspring** - What Happened To You?
15 **Lynyrd Skynyrd** - The Needle and the Spoon
16 **Neil Young** - The Needle and the Damage Done

OTHER
PLAYLISTS

17 **Mötley Crüe** - Smoke The Sky

18 **Young MC** - Just Say No

19 **Jefferson Airplane** - White Rabbit

20 **Marcy Playground** - Opium

21 **Alice in Chains** - Chemical Addiction

22 **Queens of the Stone Age** - Feel Good Hit of
the Summer

23 **The Velvet Underground** - Heroin

24 **The Verve** - The Drugs Don't Work

25 **Pitty Sing** - On Drugs

26 **Adam Ant** - Goody Two Shoes

27 **Animal Collective** - Who Could Win a Rabbit*

28 **Billy Idol** - Trouble with the Sweet Stuff

29 **The Rolling Stones** - Mother's Little Helper

30 **Eric Clapton** - Cocaine

31 **The Dead Milkmen** - Junkie

32 **Peter Tosh** - Legalize It

33 **Red Hot Chili Peppers** - Under the Bridge

* These songs are not definitely about drugs, but they
sound like it.

## DUETS

Partnering up is the way of life, and in some cases, the way it should be in songs.

01 **blink-182 with Robert Smith** - All Of This
02 **Bonnie Tyler with Rory Dodd** - Total Eclipse of the Heart
03 **Lovage** (Mike Patton and Jennifer Charles) - Sex (I'm A)
04 **Placebo with David Bowie** - Without You I'm Nothing
05 **Fat Joe with Ashanti** - What's Luv?
06 **PJ Harvey with Thom Yorke** - This Mess We're In
07 **Queen with David Bowie** - Under Pressure
08 **Billy Joel with Ray Charles** - Baby Grand
09 **Jay-Z with Beyoncé** - '03 Bonnie And Clyde
10 **Nancy Sinatra with Lee Hazlewood** - Some Velvet Morning*
11 **Bing Crosby with David Bowie** - Little Drummer Boy
12 **Loretta Lynn with Jack White** - Portland Oregon
13 **Michael Jackson with Janet Jackson** - Scream
14 **Natalie Cole with Nat King Cole** - Unforgettable**

OTHER PLAYLISTS

15 **Robbie Williams with Nicole Kidman** - Somethin' Stupid\*\*\*

16 **Smashing Pumpkins with Nina Gordon** - . . . Said Sadly

17 **Paula Abdul with MC Skat Cat** - Opposites Attract

18 **Ozzy Osbourne with Kelly Osbourne** - Changes

19 **Regina Spektor with The Strokes** - Modern Girls & Old Fashion Men

20 **Britney Spears with Madonna** - Me Against the Music

21 **Gorillaz with Shaun Ryder** - DARE

22 **Eve with Gwen Stefani** - Let Me Blow Ya Mind

23 **Kenny Rogers with Dolly Parton** - Islands in the Stream\*\*\*\*

---

\*       This song was later covered by Primal Scream with supermodel Kate Moss.

\*\*     Nat King Cole was very dead when Natalie Cole recorded her vocals and released this song.

\*\*\*   This song was originally performed by the father/daughter duo Frank and Nancy Sinatra.

\*\*\*\* This song was written by the Bee Gees and produced by Barry Gibb.

OTHER
PLAYLISTS

## ENTRANCE MUSIC

There's nothing wrong with making an entrance set to music that will make the room's climate change.

01 **Blur** - Song 2
02 **Gary Glitter** - Rock & Roll, Pt. 2
03 **The Chemical Brothers** - Hey Boy Hey Girl
04 **Coldplay** - Politik
05 **Guns N' Roses** - Welcome to the Jungle
06 **David Bowie** - Rebel Rebel
07 **Republica** - Ready to Go
08 **Deftones** - Back to School (Mini Maggit)
09 **Depeche Mode** - Personal Jesus
10 **The Doors** - Touch Me
11 **U2** - Sunday Bloody Sunday
12 **Echo & the Bunnymen** - The Killing Moon
13 **Elastica** - Connection
14 **Carl Orff** - Carmina Burana
15 **Beyoncé** - Crazy in Love
16 **Bloc Party** - Banquet
17 **C+C Music Factory** - Gonna Make You Sweat
   (Everybody Dance Now)

OTHER
PLAYLISTS

## FIGHTING SONGS

These songs will get you revved up to FIGHT! Or just compete.

01 **Led Zeppelin** - Immigrant Song
02 **AC/DC** - Highway to Hell
03 **Fugazi** - Waiting Room
04 **Blur** - Song 2
05 **Marvin Gaye** - Anger
06 **The Alarm** - The Stand
07 **The Rolling Stones** - Street Fighting Man
08 **Sex Pistols** - Anarchy in the U.K.
09 **Björk** - Army of Me
10 **APB** - Shoot You Down
11 **Death Cab for Cutie** - Army Corps of Architects
12 **Dead Kennedys** - Riot
13 **t.A.T.u.** - Not Gonna Get Us
14 **Muse** - Hysteria
15 **Survivor** - Eye of the Tiger
16 **Steppenwolf** - Born to Be Wild
17 **Soul Asylum** - Somebody to Shove
18 **Linkin Park** - One Step Closer
19 **The Walkmen** - The Rat

20 **Hole** - Asking for It

21 **The Vines** - Outtathaway!

22 **Catatonia** - Mulder and Scully

23 **Drugstore** - El President

24 **Adam and the Ants** - Stand and Deliver

25 **Republica** - Ready to Go

26 **Courtney Love** - Mono

OTHER
PLAYLISTS

## FIRST-DATE SONGS

There's nothing more nerve-racking than worrying if you're going to have fun on your first date. Don't worry, just be your cute self.

01 **Al Green** - Let's Stay Together
02 **The Troggs** - Wild Thing
03 **Aretha Franklin** - (You Make Me Feel Like) A Natural Woman
04 **Ash** - Candy
05 **The Beach Boys** - God Only Knows
06 **Suede** - Beautiful Ones
07 **AC/DC** - You Shook Me All Night Long
08 **Beck** - Where It's At
09 **Jennifer Lopez** - Waiting for Tonight
10 **Gwen Stefani** - What You Waiting For?
11 **Buzzcocks** - Ever Fallen In Love?

## FIVE A.M. AND I NEED TO SLEEP MIX

Counting sheep becomes boring after a while, not to mention the fact that it rarely works. Here are songs that will drop your heart rate, relax you, and help you drift off into a sweet slumber. This also doubles as a superrelaxing mellow mix.

01 **Radiohead** - Street Spirit (Fade Out)
02 **Björk** - Scatterheart
03 **Sigur Rós** - *Svefn-g-englar*
04 **My Morning Jacket** - Can You See The Hard Helmet On
05 **The Beatles** - Across the Universe
06 **Sneaker Pimps** - 6 Underground
07 **Brand New** - Play Crack the Sky
08 **Adam Ant** - Wonderful
09 **Air** - *La Femme d'Argent*
10 **Blur** - The Universal
11 **The Flying Burrito Brothers** - To Love Somebody
12 **Al Green** - I'm Still In Love With You
13 **Archer Prewitt** - Way of the Sun
14 **The Beatles** - Dear Prudence
15 **Beck** - Jack-ass

**OTHER PLAYLISTS**

16 **Belle & Sebastian** - I Don't Love Anyone

17 **Big Star** - Thirteen

18 **Elysian Fields** - Drunk On Dark Sublime

19 **David Bowie** - Quicksand

20 **Elliott Smith** - Miss Misery

21 **Elvis Costello & the Imposters** - Dark End of the Street (The Clarksdale Sessions)

22 **Feist** - Mushaboom

23 **The Flaming Lips** - Feeling Yourself Disintegrate

24 **Foo Fighters** - Everlong (Acoustic)

25 **Graham Coxon** - Ribbons And Leaves

26 **Iron & Wine** - Such Great Heights

27 **Jane's Addiction** - Classic Girl

28 **Jeff Buckley** - Hallelujah

29 **Joanna Newsom** - This Side of the Blue

30 **John Lennon** - Jealous Guy

31 **Karen Ann** - Not Going Anywhere

32 **The Velvet Underground** - Candy Says

33 **The Cure** - A Forest

## GAY ANTHEMS

The word "gay" means having a sexual orientation to persons of the same sex *and* it means characterized by cheerfulness and lighthearted excitement—together they equal this mix being insanely fun.

01 **The Weather Girls** - It's Raining Men
02 **Placebo** - My Sweet Prince
03 **Gwen Stefani** - What You Waiting For?
04 **Frankie Goes to Hollywood** - Relax
05 **Whitney Houston** - I Wanna Dance With Somebody (Who Loves Me)
06 **Olivia Newton-John** - Xanadu
07 **RuPaul** - Supermodel (You Better Work)
08 **George Michael** - Faith
09 **Cher** - Song for the Lonely
10 **Britney Spears** - I'm a Slave 4 U
11 **Culture Club** - Karma Chameleon

**OTHER PLAYLISTS**

## GRADUATION THEME SONGS

You made it. It may have taken more than four years, but you are finally graduating. So toss that motorboard in the air, put on these tunes, and celebrate before the shock of entering the real world sets in.

01 **Coldplay** - Warning Sign
02 **The Killers** - All These Things That I've Done
03 **Interpol** - No Exit
04 **Cyndi Lauper** - True Colors
05 **Vitamin C** - Graduation (Friends Forever)
06 **The Carpenters** - We've Only Just Begun
07 **Queen** - These Are the Days of Our Lives
08 **Indigo Girls** - Least Complicated
09 **Sheryl Crow** - All I Wanna Do
10 **Semisonic** - Closing Time
11 **Third Eye Blind** - Graduate
12 **The Used** - Taste of Ink
13 **Taking Back Sunday** - Number Five with a Bullet
14 **10,000 Maniacs** - These Are Days
15 **\*NSYNC** - Bye Bye Bye
16 **Ja'net DuBois** - Movin' On Up (*The Jeffersons* theme song)

17 **The Cure** - Just Like Heaven

18 **U2** - Walk On

19 **The Verve** - Bitter Sweet Symphony

20 **Peter Gabriel** - In Your Eyes

21 **Snow Patrol** - Run

22 **Boyz II Men** - End of the Road

23 **Green Day** - Good Riddance (Time of Your Life)

OTHER

## HUNGOVER

A few years ago I went to some *Saturday Night Live* after-after-after-party with my friend Gideon, and we were there till the sun came up. The next day I woke up on his couch to him playing the Velvet Underground's "Sunday Morning," and in my incredibly dehydrated and hungover state, I realized how wonderful it was to hear that song.

01 **The Velvet Underground** - Sunday Morning
02 **Black Rebel Motorcycle Club** - White Palms
03 **Blur** - The Universal
04 **The Brian Jonestown Massacre** - Wasted
05 **The Verve** - Sonnet
06 **British Sea Power** - Blackout
07 **Calla** - Strangler
08 **Delays** - Zero Zero One
09 **Elysian Fields** - Shooting Stars
10 **The Stone Roses** - Waterfall
11 **The Oohlas** - The Rapid
12 **Lou Reed** - Perfect Day
13 **a-ha** - Hunting High and Low
14 **Black Rebel Motorcycle Club** - Salvation
15 **Bloc Party** - So Here We Are

OTHER

## I QUIT

Finding the nerve to leave your job can be so insanely scary. But you can do it. You can do it! Be confident. Be strong. Don't back down.

01 **Sparks** - Angst in My Pants
02 **The Bangles** - Manic Monday
03 **Dolly Parton** - 9 to 5
04 **Butthole Surfers** - I Hate My Job
05 **Johnny Paycheck** - Take This Job and Shove It
06 **Prince** - Let's Work
07 **Loverboy** - Working for the Weekend
08 **R.E.M.** - Bad Day
09 **The Allman Brothers Band** - Whipping Post
10 **The White Stripes** - Hello Operator
11 **Beck** - Lost Cause
12 **Bob Dylan** - One More Cup of Coffee
13 **David Bowie** - Golden Years
14 **Cake** - I Will Survive

OTHER

## KARAOKE JAMS

You don't want to be a total chump the next time you go to karaoke, standing there reading the teleprompter, singing off-key, missing notes, missing lines. Practice makes perfect, and these songs are definite crowd-pleasers.

01 **Bon Jovi** - You Give Love a Bad Name
02 **Queen** - Bohemian Rhapsody
03 **George Michael** - Faith
04 **The Beatles** - Oh! Darling
05 **Laura Branigan** - Gloria
06 **The Darkness** - I Believe in a Thing Called Love
07 **Quiet Riot** - Cum on Feel the Noize
08 **Bonnie Tyler** - Total Eclipse of the Heart
09 **The Human League** - Don't You Want Me
10 **Elton John** - I Guess That's Why They Call It the Blues
11 **Bon Jovi** - Livin' on a Prayer
12 **Skid Row** - 18 and Life
13 **Billy Idol** - White Wedding
14 **Meat Loaf** - Paradise by the Dashboard Light
15 **Prince** - Purple Rain

OTHER

16 **Prince or Sinéad O'Connor** - Nothing Compares 2 U

17 **Don Henley** - Boys of Summer

18 **Rick James** - Super Freak

19 **Led Zeppelin** - Babe I'm Gonna Leave You

20 **Radiohead** - Creep

21 **Billy Joel** - Movin' Out

22 **Björk** - It's Oh So Quiet

23 **Frank Sinatra** - New York, New York

24 **Bon Jovi** - Wanted Dead or Alive

25 **Bruce Springsteen** - Dancing in the Dark

26 **Pat Benatar** - Love Is a Battlefield

27 **David Lee Roth** - Just a Gigolo/I Ain't Got Nobody

28 **Van Halen** - Hot for Teacher

29 **The Police** - Roxanne

30 **Pixies** - Monkey Gone to Heaven

31 **Weezer** - Say It Ain't So

OTHER
PLAYLISTS

## LIFE IS AWESOME

Some days your day is just so good that you want to dance around your room hugging your pillow and bopping your head from side to side.

01 **Arcade Fire** - Neighborhood #3 (Power Out)
02 **Joan Jett and the Blackhearts** - Bad Reputation
03 **Chumbawamba** - Tubthumping
04 **Yeah Yeah Yeahs** - Date With the Night
05 **Wilco** - Can't Stand It
06 **The White Stripes** - Fell in Love With a Girl
07 **Violent Femmes** - Blister in the Sun
08 **The Vines** - Highly Evolved
09 **Baby Bird** - You're Gorgeous
10 **U2** - New Year's Day
11 **Third Eye Blind** - Wounded
12 **Ace of Base** - Beautiful Life
13 **The All-American Rejects** - Swing, Swing
14 **Animal Collective** - Who Could Win a Rabbit
15 **Republica** - Ready to Go
16 **Big Audio Dynamite** - Rush
17 **Blondie** - Dreaming
18 **The Coral** - Dreaming of You
19 **Delays** - Lost in a Melody

20 **Cyndi Lauper** - Girls Just Want to Have Fun

21 **Beyoncé** - Crazy in Love

22 **Billy Idol** - Dancing With Myself

23 **Björk** - Violently Happy

24 **C+C Music Factory** - Gonna Make You Sweat
   (Everybody Dance Now)

**OTHER PLAYLISTS**

## NAMES IN SONGS

Serenade your loved ones by singing their names.
I promise you, they'll never get sick of it . . .
until after the fiftieth time.

01 **Erykah Badu** - Tyrone
02 **Dolly Parton** - Jolene
03 **Prince** - Darling Nikki
04 **Hall & Oates** - Sara Smile
05 **Elliott Smith** - Sweet Adeline
06 **The Police** - Roxanne
07 **Marvin Gaye** - Anna's Song
08 **Rick Springfield** - Jessie's Girl
09 **Barry Manilow** - Mandy
10 **Silverchair** - Ana's Song
11 **Adam Green** - Jessica
12 **The Allman Brothers Band** - Melissa
13 **Aerosmith** - Janie's Got a Gun
14 **Annie** - Anniemal
15 **Aretha Franklin** - Eleanor Rigby
16 **Ash** - Nicole
17 **Jellyfish** - Calling Sarah
18 **The Beach Boys** - Caroline No
19 **Siouxsie and the Banshees** - Dear Prudence

20 **Beulah** - I Love John, She Loves Paul
21 **Björk** - Isobel
22 **Blur** - Tracy Jacks
23 **Bob Dylan** - Sara
24 **Bouncing Souls** - Joe Lies (When He Cries)
25 **Bright Eyes** - Emily, Sing Something Sweet
26 **The Clash** - Janie Jones
27 **The Creation** - Sweet Helen
28 **Cowboy Junkies** - Sweet Jane
29 **The Creation** - Hey Joe
30 **The Cure** - Charlotte Sometimes
31 **Dolly Parton** - Joshua
32 **Elastica** - Annie
33 **Elefant** - Annie
34 **Elvis Costello** - Alison

**OTHER PLAYLISTS**

## OUTER SPACE JAMS

You're camping, you've got your MP3 player with you, and you're dreaming of floating off into the stars to hang out with moon men. Here are your jams!

01 **Marvin Gaye** - A Funky Space Reincarnation
02 **Seu Jorge** - Life on Mars?
03 **David Bowie** - Space Oddity
04 **Modest Mouse** - Space Travel Is Boring
05 **Muse** - Space Dementia
06 **Pixies** - Space (I Believe In)
07 **Smashing Pumpkins** - Spaceboy
08 **The Verve** - Space and Time
09 **Weezer** - Space Rock
10 **Billie Holiday** - Blue Moon
11 **Echo & the Bunnymen** - The Killing Moon
12 **Love and Rockets** - Earth, Sun, Moon
13 **The Magnetic Fields** - You and Me and the Moon
14 **Morrissey** - Moon River
15 **Neko Case** - I Wish I Was the Moon
16 **Nick Drake** - Pink Moon
17 **Prince** - Under the Cherry Moon
18 **Radiohead** - Subterranean Homesick Alien

19 **Duran Duran** - New Moon On Monday
20 **David Bowie** - Life on Mars?
21 **Ash** - Girl From Mars
22 **TV on the Radio** - Staring at the Sun
23 **T. Rex** - Cosmic Dancer

**OTHER PLAYLISTS**

## OUTFIT CHANGE

Clothes-changing montages are cheesy on TV, so why not in real life?

01 **ABBA** - Dancing Queen
02 **Paula Abdul** - Straight Up
03 **Dizzee Rascal** - Fix Up, Look Sharp
04 **Shirley Ellis** - The Clapping Song (Clap Pat Clap Slap)
05 **Roy Ayers** - Running Away
06 **Grandmaster Flash and the Furious Five** - The Message
07 **Missy Elliott** - Work It
08 **Destiny's Child** - Bootylicious
09 **George Michael** - Freedom 90
10 **AC/DC** - Back in Black
11 **Björk** - Big Time Sensuality
12 **Joan Jett and the Blackhearts** - Bad Reputation
13 **No Doubt** - Hey Baby
14 **Bee Gees** - Stayin' Alive
15 **Rick Astley** - Never Gonna Give You Up
16 **Ramones** - Blitzkrieg Bop
17 **Kylie Minogue** - Can't Get You Out of My Head
18 **The Weather Girls** - It's Raining Men

## PLANE RIDE TO VISIT YOUR EX

Save the Xanax for the ride home and listen to this mix instead.

01 **Adam Green** - We're Not Supposed to Be Lovers
02 **Aerosmith** - Dream On
03 **Avril Lavigne** - My Happy Ending
04 **Radiohead** - Street Spirit (Fade Out)
05 **blink-182** - All of This
06 **Blondie** - Dreaming
07 **Brand New** - The Boy Who Blocked His Own Shot
08 **British Sea Power** - Something Wicked
09 **The Cardigans** - My Favourite Game
10 **Justin Timberlake** - Cry Me a River
11 **The English Beat** - Save It for Later
12 **Bananarama** - Cruel Summer
13 **Yaz** - Don't Go
14 **Elvis Presley** - Are You Lonesome Tonight?

## PLAY LOUD TO ANNOY YOUR ROOMMATE

Did your roommate forget that it was his turn to take out the garbage or do the dishes? Don't stand for that—play some music really loud until he gets the idea that you are not pleased.

01 **Styx** - Come Sail Away
02 **Meat Loaf** - Paradise by the Dashboard Light
03 **Nirvana** - Smells Like Teen Spirit
04 **Journey** - Any Way You Want It
05 **ABBA** - Dancing Queen
06 **Foreigner** - Cold As Ice
07 **Refused** - New Noise
08 **Kelis** - Milkshake
09 **The Vines** - Get Free
10 **Hole** - Olympia
11 **Queen** - Bohemian Rhapsody
12 **The Allman Brothers Band** - Jessica
13 **Los Lobos** - La Bamba
14 **Jay-Z** - 99 Problems
15 **C+C Music Factory** - Gonna Make You Sweat (Everybody Dance Now)
16 **Ace of Base** - All That She Wants
17 **Jet** - Are You Gonna Be My Girl

18 **Eddy Grant** - Electric Avenue

19 **Wang Chung** - Everybody Have Fun Tonight

20 **Britney Spears** - Toxic

21 **Backstreet Boys** - Everybody (Backstreet's Back)

22 **Stereophonics** - Hangbags and Gladrags

23 **Maroon 5** - This Love

24 **Fastball** - The Way

25 **Sugar Ray** - Fly

26 **Limp Bizkit** - Nookie

27 **Gin Blossoms** - Hey Jealousy

28 **Spin Doctors** - Two Princes

29 **Shania Twain** - That Don't Impress Me Much

30 **Us3** - Cantaloop

31 **The Proclaimers** - I'm Gonna Be (500 Miles)

32 **R.E.M.** - Shiny Happy People

33 **Georgia Satellites** - Keep Your Hands to Yourself

**OTHER PLAYLISTS**

## POOL PARTY

This is the longest mix for a few reasons:

1. If you are soaking wet from swimming in a pool, it is a very bad idea to operate electronic equipment. Just press play and you've got nonstop amazing music for a few hours.
2. Pool parties will often last all afternoon.
3. For those without a pool, this mix will still work for you. (Also works well when shuffled.)

01 **Adam and the Ants** - Beat My Guest
02 **Annie** - Heartbeat
03 **Arcade Fire** - Neighborhood #1 (Tunnels)
04 **Ash** - Girl From Mars
05 **The B-52's** - 52 Girls
06 **Basement Jaxx** - Red Alert
07 **Beastie Boys** - So What'cha Want
08 **The Beatles** - Tomorrow Never Knows
09 **Beck** - E-Pro
10 **Bee Gees** - Stayin' Alive
11 **Belle & Sebastian** - Legal Man
12 **Brendan Benson** - Spit It Out
13 **Beyoncé** - Crazy in Love
14 **Bloc Party** - Banquet

15 **Blur** - Girls & Boys
16 **David Bowie** - Rebel Rebel
17 **Neneh Cherry** - Buffalo Stance
18 **The Clash** - Rock the Casbah
19 **The Coral** - Dreaming of You
20 **The Cult** - She Sells Sanctuary
21 **Culture Club** - Karma Chameleon
22 **The Cure** - Friday I'm in Love
23 **Daft Punk** - Robot Rock
24 **The Dandy Warhols** - Bohemian Like You
25 **Devo** - Girl U Want
26 **Duran Duran** - Girls on Film
27 **Bob Dylan** - Subterranean Homesick Blues
28 **The Flaming Lips** - She Don't Use Jelly
29 **Franz Ferdinand** - Jacqueline
30 **Fugazi** - Waiting Room
31 **The Futureheads** - Hounds of Love
32 **Peter Gabriel** - Sledgehammer
33 **Gang of Four** - Damaged Goods
34 **The Go! Team** - The Power Is On
35 **Go-Go's** - We Got the Beat
36 **Gorillaz** - Feel Good Inc.
37 **Guns N' Roses** - Live and Let Die
38 **Heart** - Barracuda

**OTHER PLAYLISTS**

39 **The Human League** - Don't You Want Me

40 **Michael Jackson** - Don't Stop 'Til You Get Enough

41 **The Jesus and Mary Chain** - Just Like Honey

42 **Joy Division** - Love Will Tear Us Apart

43 **Kaiser Chiefs** - I Predict a Riot

44 **Kings of Leon** - California Waiting

45 **KISS** - Detroit Rock City

46 **LCD Soundsystem** - Daft Punk Is Playing at My House

47 **Led Zeppelin** - Immigrant Song

48 **LL Cool J** - Going Back to Cali

49 **M.I.A.** - Galang

50 **George Michael** - Freedom 90

51 **The Modern Lovers** - Road Runner

52 **Morrissey** - Suedehead

53 **New Order** - True Faith-'94

54 **Nirvana** - Sliver

55 **Pet Shop Boys** - West End Girls

56 **Pixies** - Debaser

57 **Placebo** - Pure Morning

58 **Plastic Bertrand** - *Ça plane pour moi*

59 **The Postal Service** - Such Great Heights

60 **Primal Scream** - Movin' on Up

OTHER PLAYLISTS

61 **Prince** - Let's Go Crazy

62 **Pulp** - Disco 2000

63 **Queen** - Another One Bites the Dust

64 **Queens of the Stone Age** - Feel Good Hit of the Summer

65 **R.E.M.** - (Don't Go Back to) Rockville

66 **Radiohead** - Idioteque

67 **Ramones** - Sheena Is a Punk Rocker

68 **The Rapture** - House of Jealous Lovers

69 **The Raveonettes** - Chain Gang of Love

70 **The Rolling Stones** - Rocks Off

71 **Run-D.M.C.** - It's Tricky

72 **Salt 'N Pepa** - Push It

73 **Screaming Trees** - Nearly Lost You

74 **Shannon** - Let the Music Play

75 **The Smiths** - Bigmouth Strikes Again

76 **Stereo MC's** - Connected

77 **The Stone Roses** - Fools Gold

78 **The Stooges** - I Wanna Be Your Dog

79 **The Strokes** - Hard to Explain

80 **Supergrass** - Rush Hour Soul

81 **Survivor** - Eye of the Tiger

82 **Sweet** - Ballroom Blitz

83 **Tears for Fears** - Shout

**OTHER PLAYLISTS**

84 **Tones on Tail** - Go!

85 **TV on the Radio** - Staring at the Sun

86 **U2** - New Year's Day

87 **Underworld** - Born Slippy

88 **Van Halen** - Panama

89 **The White Stripes** - The Hardest Button to Button

90 **The Who** - I Can't Explain

## POOPING SONGS

You don't want anyone to know what you're up to in there, do you?

01 **Coldplay** - Yellow
02 **Pixies** - Here Comes Your Man
03 **Interpol** - Slow Hands (Dan the Automator Remix)
04 **Sex Pistols** - Pretty Vacant
05 **Weezer** - Say It Ain't So
06 **Nina Simone** - Work Song
07 **Primal Scream** - Come Together
08 **Pink** - There You Go
09 **Jay-Z** - 99 Problems
10 **Rival Schools** - Good Things
11 **A Tribe Called Quest** - Scenario
12 **The Cure** - In Between Days
13 **The La's** - There She Goes

OTHER
PLAYLISTS

## PROM-THEMED PARTY

Either you didn't attend your prom, or it sucked, or it ruled so hard that you want to relive it over and over again in post-ironic prom-themed parties.

01 **Alphaville** - Forever Young
02 **Violent Femmes** - Blister in the Sun
03 **a-ha** - Take On Me
04 **Styx** - Come Sail Away
05 **REO Speedwagon** - Keep on Loving You
06 **KISS** - Beth
07 **Journey** - Don't Stop Believin'
08 **Bobby Brown** - My Prerogative
09 **Asia** - Heat of the Moment
10 **Alice Cooper** - School's Out

OTHER
PLAYLISTS

## ROOT CANAL

There is only one album that I can fully recommend with complete backing for this category. When I was twenty-one, I had to get two root canals. It was terribly painful, and all I wanted was to be lifted off into another place, another space, another time. This album made me feel like I was floating in the clouds having conversations with angels in a language I couldn't speak but could understand. It must have been the excessive Novocain. Here are the tracks from the album *Ágætis Byrjun* by Sigur Rós:

01 Intro
02 *Svefn-g-englar*
03 *Starálfur*
04 *Flugufrelsarinn*
05 *Ný batterí*
06 *Hjartað hamast*
07 *Viðrar vel til loftárása*
08 *Olsen Olsen*
09 *Ágætis byrjun*
10 Avalon

OTHER
PLAYLISTS

## SAD SONGS

Sometimes I'm so happy that I have to balance it out with some of the saddest, most heartbreaking songs I know. You know, just to remind me that there are other emotions in this world.

01 **Interpol** - Untitled
02 **Death Cab for Cutie** - Transatlanticism
03 **Spaceman 3** - Fixin' to Die
04 **Blur** - Out of Time
05 **Echo & the Bunnymen** - The Killing Moon
06 **INXS** - Never Tear Us Apart
07 **Morrissey** - Whatever Happens, I Love You
08 **Nada Surf** - Inside of Love
09 **Nine Inch Nails** - Something I Can Never Have
10 **Pulp** - This Is Hardcore
11 **Yeah Yeah Yeahs** - Maps
12 **The Smiths** - Asleep

OTHER
PLAYLISTS

## SEND IN THE CLOWNS

Clowns inspire an inexplicable fear in lots of people. So naturally, you should have a mix handy to freak these people out (including all seven versions of "Send in the Clowns.")

01 **Barbra Streisand** - Send in the Clowns
02 **Cold** - Send in the Clowns
03 **Diana Ross** - Send in the Clowns
04 **Frank Sinatra** - Send in the Clowns
05 **Krusty the Clown** - Send in the Clowns
06 **Grace Jones** - Send in the Clowns
07 **Perry Como** - Send in the Clowns
08 **Dead Kennedys** - Rambozo the Clown
09 **The Beatnuts** - You're a Clown
10 **Cocteau Twins** - Fifty-Fifty Clown
11 **Graham Parker** - They Murdered the Clown
12 **Sugar** - Clownmaster
13 **Shawn Mullins** - Drumming Clown
14 **Sarah McLachlan** - Sad Clowns
15 **Elvis Costello** - Clown Strike
16 **Frank Zappa** - Clowns on Velvet
17 **G. Love & Special Sauce** - Rodeo Clowns
18 **Insane Clown Posse** - Clown Love

OTHER

19 **Oingo Boingo** - Clowns of Death

20 **Korn** - Clown

21 **Mariah Carey** - Clown

22 **t.A.T.u.** - Clowns (Can You See Me Now?)

23 **Roy Orbison** - The Clown

24 **Saint Etienne** - Here Come Clown Feet

25 **Reba McEntire** - Cathy's Clown

## SLOW DANCE

Impromptu slow dances happen ALL THE TIME. Right? Here's a playlist so you're prepared the next time that happens!

01 **Mazzy Star** - Fade Into You
02 **Chris de Burgh** - The Lady in Red
03 **Kelly Clarkson** - A Moment Like This
04 **Phil Collins** - Against All Odds (Take a Look at Me Now)
05 **Elvis Presley** - Always on My Mind
06 **Wham!** - Careless Whisper
07 **Elton John** - Can You Feel the Love Tonight
08 **Al Green** - Let's Stay Together
09 **Seal** - Love's Divine
10 **Billy Joel** - Just the Way You Are
11 **Cyndi Lauper** - Time After Time
12 **Foreigner** - Waiting for a Girl Like You
13 **Nat King Cole** - Unforgettable
14 **Elefant** - Tonight Let's Dance
15 **Mandy Moore** - I Wanna Be With You
16 **ABC** - The Look of Love
17 **Bryan Adams** - (Everything I Do) I Do It for You
18 **Bad English** - When I See You Smile

OTHER

## SONGS FOR MOURNING

Losing a loved one is never easy. These songs will empathize with you when nobody else will.

01 **Barbra Streisand** - Memory (theme from *Cats*)
02 **The Beach Boys** - God Only Knows (Stereo Mix)
03 **The Beatles** - Yesterday
04 **Blur** - Beetlebum
05 **The Smiths** - Cemetery Gates
06 **Jeff Buckley** - Hallelujah
07 **R.E.M.** - Everybody Hurts
08 **Cyndi Lauper** - Time After Time
09 **Radiohead** - Sulk
10 **Nirvana** - All Apologies
11 **Nine Inch Nails** - Hurt
12 **Morrissey** - Moon River
13 **Björk** - Hyper-Ballad
14 **Radiohead** - Bullet Proof . . . I Wish I Was
15 **Interpol** - The New
16 **Arcade Fire** - In the Backseat
17 **My Chemical Romance** - Cemetery Drive
18 **Moby** - Porcelain
19 **Silverchair** - Cemetery
20 **Rival Schools** - Undercovers On

OTHER

## SONGS FOR YOUR HAUNTED HOUSE

These are either the worst songs to play if you think your house is haunted or the best—if you totally like messing with those otherworldly menaces.

01 **Air** - Ghost Song
02 **Mazzy Star** - Ghost Highway
03 **Joy Division** - Dead Souls
04 **Rockwell** - Somebody's Watching Me
05 **Michael Jackson** - Thriller
06 **Placebo** - Sleeping With Ghosts
07 **My Chemical Romance** - The Ghost of You
08 **Controller.Controller** - Silent Seven
09 **The Psychedelic Furs** - The Ghost in You
10 **British Sea Power** - Something Wicked
11 **Louis XIV** - The Ghost of the Chapel Royal
12 **Blue Öyster Cult** - (Don't Fear) The Reaper
13 **Pixies** - Monkey Gone to Heaven
14 **Good Charlotte** - Ghost of You
15 **The Oohlas** - The Ballerina Blues
16 **Blur** - Death of a Party
17 **HIM** - When Love and Death Embrace
18 **Neutral Milk Hotel** - Ghost
19 **The Raveonettes** - Attack of the Ghost Riders

OTHER
PLAYLISTS

20 **Led Zeppelin** - Stairway to Heaven

21 **The Specials** - Ghost Town

22 **Bloc Party** - She's Hearing Voices

23 **Tegan and Sara** - Walking With a Ghost

24 **Talking Heads** - Psycho Killer

25 **Love and Rockets** - Everybody Wants to
Go to Heaven

26 **Ray Parker Jr.** - Ghostbusters

27 **Bauhaus** - Bela Lugosi's Dead

28 **Metric** - Dead Disco

29 **Queens of the Stone Age** - A Song for the Dead

## SONGS TO GET SPANKED BY

Bend over, pull down your pants, and call up your man to come over and test this one out.

01 **Devo** - Whip It
02 **Depeche Mode** - Master and Servant
03 **Lords of Acid** - I Sit on Acid
04 **Adam and the Ants** - Beat My Guest
05 **Læther Strip** - Fit for Flogging
06 **Ministry** - Breathe
07 **Die Form** - Sex by Force
08 **My Life With The Thrill Kill Kult** - Leathersex
09 **Blur** - Girls & Boys
10 **Nine Inch Nails** - Get Down, Make Love
11 **Noise Unit** - Dominator
12 **Justify My Love (The Beast Within Mix)** - Madonna
13 **Marilyn Manson** - Cake and Sodomy
14 **K.C. & the Sunshine Band** - That's The Way (I Like It)
15 **Apoptygma Berzerk** - Non-Stop Violence
16 **Peaches** - Fuck the Pain Away
17 **:wumpscut:** - I Want You
18 **The Prodigy** - Smack My Bitch Up

19 **Soft Cell** - Sex Dwarf

20 **Skinny Puppy** - Far Too Frail

21 **KMFDM** - Disobedience

22 **Frankie Goes to Hollywood** - Relax

23 **Icicle Works** - Whisper to a Scream (Birds Fly)

## SONGS TO GET YOUR THIRTEEN-YEAR-OLD COUSIN INTO GOOD MUSIC

Do you remember when your older cousin yelled at you for listening to whatever song you were obsessing over by saying, "Ugh, this sounds like a total rip off of a band that is way better"? Sometimes he was right. Here are some artists that your thirteen-year-old cousin probably likes, paired off with their influences (aka awesome bands that you liked first).

01 **The Killers** - Jenny Was a Friend of Mine (The Smiths - Stop Me If You Think You've Heard This One Before)

02 **Muse** - Time Is Running Out (Queen - Bohemian Rhapsody)

03 **Coldplay** - Yellow (Echo & the Bunnymen - Bring on the Dancing Horses)

04 **Radiohead** - Paranoid Android (Pink Floyd - Wish You Were Here)

05 **Franz Ferdinand** - Take Me Out (Talking Heads - Road to Nowhere)

06 **Interpol** - Not Even Jail (Joy Division - Love Will Tear Us Apart)

OTHER
PLAYLISTS

07 **Bloc Party** - She's Hearing Voices (Gang of Four - To Hell With Poverty!)

08 **Kasabian** - Club Foot (Primal Scream - Swastika Eyes)

09 **The Libertines** - I Get Along (The Clash - Janie Jones)

10 **Brand New** - The Quiet Things That No One Ever Knows (Morrissey - Whatever Happens, I Love You)

11 **Jet** - Are You Gonna Be My Girl (Iggy Pop - Lust for Life)

12 **Jet** - Rollover DJ (AC/DC - Back in Black)

OTHER

## SONGS TO HELP YOU LOSE THOSE EXTRA POUNDS

Step up to the treadmill, strap on your head-phones, and pray that nobody notices you singing along or pumping your fist into the air. This mix also works well if you need to psych yourself up for a battle, which is everyday, I'm sure.

01 **Led Zeppelin** - Immigrant Song
02 **AC/DC** - Highway to Hell
03 **Fugazi** - Waiting Room
04 **Blur** - Song 2
05 **The Alarm** - The Stand
06 **The Rolling Stones** - Street Fighting Man
07 **Sex Pistols** - Anarchy in the U.K.
08 **Van Halen** - Jump
09 **Marky Mark and the Funky Bunch** - Good Vibrations
10 **Björk** - Army of Me
11 **C+C Music Factory** - Gonna Make You Sweat (Everybody Dance Now)
12 **APB** - Shoot You Down
13 **Death Cab for Cutie** - Army Corps of Architects

OTHER

14 **Dead Kennedys** - Riot
15 **t.A.T.u.** - Not Gonna Get Us
16 **Muse** - Hysteria
17 **Survivor** - Eye of the Tiger
18 **Steppenwolf** - Born to Be Wild
19 **Soul Asylum** - Somebody to Shove
20 **Linkin Park** - One Step Closer
21 **The Walkmen** - The Rat
22 **Hole** - Asking for It
23 **Billy Idol** - Mony Mony
24 **The Vines** - Outtathaway!
25 **Adam and the Ants** - Stand and Deliver
26 **Republica** - Ready to Go
27 **Courtney Love** - Mono

OTHER

## SONGS TO TUNE OUT YOUR CHATTY COWORKERS

Yap, yap, yap—all day long. Every office has at least one Chatty Cathy who won't shut up and let you do your work so you can get out of there at a decent hour. Get your headphones out and they'll magically disappear as you float off into work land.

01 **Bananarama** - Cruel Summer
02 **The Beach Boys** - Wouldn't It Be Nice
03 **R.E.M.** - It's the End of the World as We Know It (and I Feel Fine)
04 **Snow Patrol** - Run
05 **Coldplay** - Don't Panic
06 **Patsy Cline** - Crazy
07 **The Proclaimers** - I'm Gonna Be (500 Miles)
08 **James Brown** - I Feel Good
09 **Björk** - Hyper-Ballad
10 **Third Eye Blind** - Semi-Charmed Life
11 **Lit** - My Own Worst Enemy
12 **New Order** - Blue Monday
13 **Devo** - Working in the Coal Mine
14 **ABBA** - Money, Money, Money
15 **Duran Duran** - Rio

OTHER PLAYLISTS

## SONGS YOU LIKE THAT YOUR PARENTS WILL LIKE TOO

Car rides with your parents can be excruciating when you're stuck listening to their really bad taste in music because they're convinced that you just listen to garbage. Prove them wrong.

01 **The Beach Boys** - God Only Knows
02 **Morrissey** - The More You Ignore Me, the Closer I Get
03 **Bloc Party** - So Here We Are
04 **Coldplay** - Yellow
05 **Travis** - Why Does it Always Rain on Me?
06 **Arcade Fire** - In the Backseat
07 **Jet** - Look What You've Done
08 **The Flaming Lips** - Do You Realize??
09 **Tal Bachman** - She's So High
10 **a-ha** - The Sun Always Shines on TV
11 **Yeah Yeah Yeahs** - Maps
12 **Nirvana** - All Apologies

OTHER
PLAYLISTS

## SORRY ABOUT THE CRABS

Uh-oh. You made a terrible mistake and you need
to make it up to her. Try this . . . for starters.

01 **Ashlee Simpson** - Sorry
02 **Elton John** - Sorry Seems to Be the Hardest
   Word
03 **Simple Plan** - Perfect
04 **Ruben Studdard** - Sorry 2004
05 **Third Eye Blind** - Wounded
06 **Ash** - Burn Baby Burn
07 **Bauhaus** - Burning From the Inside
08 **The Beatles** - Yesterday
09 **Black Rebel Motorcycle Club** - Love Burns
10 **The Bravery** - An Honest Mistake
11 **Bright Eyes** - Lover I Don't Have to Love
12 **Fiona Apple** - Criminal

## SORRY YOUR DAD IS GAY

We've all been there before: You are convinced your parents don't have sex anymore because it's really gross to imagine. What you didn't realize is that your dad is gay. Gay as the day is long. Shocker. But don't worry, these songs will help you out.

01 **The White Stripes** - Hardest Button to Button
02 **The Killers** - Everything Will Be Alright
03 **Scissor Sisters** - Mary
04 **Erasure** - A Little Respect
05 **Cyndi Lauper** - Girls Just Want to Have Fun
06 **Peter Gabriel** - Shock the Monkey
07 **The Weather Girls** - It's Raining Men
08 **Right Said Fred** - I'm Too Sexy
09 **RuPaul** - Supermodel (You Better Work)
10 **Pet Shop Boys** - It's a Sin
11 **Pulp** - This Is Hardcore
12 **Cheap Trick** - Surrender
13 **Jimmy Eat World** - Believe in What You Want
14 **Acceptance** - Take Cover
15 **Morrissey** - America Is Not the World
16 **Björk** - Big Time Sensuality

17 **Nirvana** - Come As You Are
18 **R.A. the Rugged Man** - Chains
19 **The Bloodhound Gang** - I Wish I Was Queer So I Could Get Chicks
20 **Mike and the Mechanics** - Living Years

OTHER
PLAYLISTS

## STAY IN LOVE WITH ME

Songs for the one you love, who loves you back.

01 **The Beach Boys** - God Only Knows
02 **The Beatles** - I Want to Hold Your Hand
03 **Elvis Presley** - Can't Help Falling in Love
04 **Radiohead** - Punchdrunk Lovesick Singalong
05 **David Bowie** - Modern Love
06 **Suede** - Beautiful Ones
07 **Stevie Wonder** - I Believe (When I Fall in Love It Will Be Forever)
08 **Björk** - Violently Happy
09 **Arcade Fire** - Neighborhood #1 (Tunnels)
10 **Blondie** - Picture This
11 **The Cure** - Lovesong
12 **R.E.M.** - The One I Love
13 **The Partridge Family** - I Woke Up in Love This Morning
14 **Blur** - Tender
15 **Beyoncé** - Crazy in Love
16 **The Used** - I Caught Fire
17 **Justin Timberlake** - Like I Love You
18 **The Mamas & the Papas** - Dedicated to the One I Love

19 **Buzzcocks** - Ever Fallen In Love?

20 **Echo & the Bunnymen** - Empire State Halo

21 **Savage Garden** - I Knew I Loved You

22 **Interpol** - C'mere

23 **Blur** - You're So Great

24 **Björk** - All Is Full of Love

25 **The Beatles** - Love Me Do

26 **The White Stripes** - Fell in Love With a Girl

## UNCONVENTIONAL CHRISTMAS SONGS

It's Christmastime and your parents are trimming the tree and drinking eggnog and killing your head with the same silly carols over and over again. You can retreat to your room with this mix and still stay in the spirit of the holidays, or maybe start a new tradition that includes better tunes.

01 **Darlene Love** - Christmas (Baby Please Come Home)
02 **The Waitresses** - Christmas Wrapping
03 **Band Aid** - Do They Know It's Christmas?
04 **Run-D.M.C.** - Christmas in Hollis
05 **Aimee Mann & Michael Penn** - Christmas Time
06 **The Kinks** - Father Christmas
07 **Big Dee Irwin and Little Eva** - I Wish You A Merry Christmas
08 **Bing Crosby and David Bowie** - Peace On Earth/Little Drummer Boy
09 **Ramones** - Merry Christmas (I Don't Want to Fight Tonight)
10 **Slade** - Merry Xmas Everybody
11 **Phil Spector** - Silent Night
12 **Idlewild** - The Bronze Medal
13 **Bright Eyes** - Little Drummer Boy

## UNDERAGE ANTHEMS

I totally know that homework sucks, and that mom's a drag sometimes, and that you want to be treated like an adult, but you need to stop dating those girls in high school first!

01 **Interpol** - Not Even Jail
02 **Aaliyah** - Age Ain't Nothing but a Number
03 **Louis XIV** - Illegal Tender
04 **Simple Plan** - I'm Just a Kid
05 **Fountains of Wayne** - Stacy's Mom
06 **Travis** - U16 Girls
07 **Ladytron** - Seventeen
08 **New Kids on the Block** - Please Don't Go Girl
09 **Donny Osmond** - Puppy Love
10 **Rick James** - Super Freak
11 **Warrant** - Cherry Pie
12 **Winger** - Seventeen
13 **The Runaways** - Cherry Bomb
14 **The Beatles** - I Saw Her Standing There
15 **Aqua** - Barbie Girl
16 **Chaka Khan** - I'm Every Woman
17 **Lindsay Lohan** - Rumors
18 **Beastie Boys** - Fight for Your Right

OTHER PLAYLISTS

## VALENTINE'S DAY ALONE

Nothing is better than feeling sorry for yourself—there's even a whole genre of music called emo that is based on the concept. For those who love to feel unloved on the day that reminds us more than any other that we're all alone, I bring you the following songs that will make you sing "woe is me" while you eat every last morsel in that heart-shaped Valentine's Day box of chocolates you bought yourself.

01 **ABC** - Poison Arrow
02 **Bauhaus** - The Passion of Lovers
03 **The Beatles** - While My Guitar Gently Weeps
04 **Beck** - Loser
05 **Morrissey** - The More You Ignore Me, the Closer I Get
06 **Billy Idol** - Dancing With Myself
07 **Blondie** - Dreaming
08 **Brand New** - The Quiet Things That No One Ever Knows
09 **British Sea Power** - Blackout
10 **The Killers** - The Ballad of Michael Valentine

11 **Space** - Female of the Species

12 **The White Stripes** - Union Forever

13 **Radiohead** - Creep

14 **The Libertines** - Can't Stand Me Now

**OTHER PLAYLISTS**

# VIRGINITY-LOSS SONGS (REALISTIC) or SONGS TO PLAY DURING A QUICKIE

A dude losing his virginity is like a water balloon that you left a wee bit too long on the faucet: Any minute he's gonna blow. So, just in case you're expecting this to take about two and a half minutes, here are some under-three-minute song gems to ensure your good time has a good soundtrack.

01 **Serge Gainsbourg** - *Ballade de Melody Nelson*
02 **Blur** - Song 2
03 **Pixies** - Wave of Mutilation
04 **Buzzcocks** - Orgasm Addict
05 **The White Stripes** - Expecting
06 **The Smiths** - Sweet and Tender Hooligan
07 **Yeah Yeah Yeahs** - Pin
08 **The Beatles** - Can't Buy Me Love
09 **The Vines** - Get Free
10 **James Brown** - Papa's Got a Brand New Bag
11 **Blondie** - I'm Gonna Love You Too
12 **Operation Ivy** - Missionary
13 **The Runaways** - Lovers
14 **Mazzy Star** - Before I Sleep

15 **The Misfits** - Fiend Club
16 **Bright Eyes** - The City Has Sex
17 **Elvis Presley** - Hound Dog
18 **The Von Bondies** - C'mon C'mon
19 **Bikini Kill** - I Like Fucking
20 **Franz Ferdinand** - Tell Her Tonight
21 **Louis XIV** - God Killed the Queen
22 **The Coral** - Dreaming of You
23 **Louis Armstrong** - What a Wonderful World
24 **Elastica** - Connection
25 **Led Zeppelin** - Immigrant Song
26 **Violent Femmes** - Blister in the Sun
27 **McLusky** - To Hell With Good Intentions
28 **The Beach Boys** - Wouldn't It Be Nice
29 **Razorlight** - Rip It Up
30 **Ramones** - I Wanna Be Your Boyfriend
31 **Dusty Springfield** - Son of a Preacher Man
32 **The Doors** - Break on Through (to the Other Side)

Oh well, at least that's out of the way now.

## VIRGINITY-LOSS SONGS (ROMANTIC) or JUST PLAIN SEXY

Seriously, this is like the most important moment of your life. There is only one album that is the best album to lose your virginity to, and that's My Bloody Valentine's *Loveless*, with Massive Attack's *Mezzanine* coming in a close second. However, if you refuse to take that advice, here are some songs you can put into a playlist for bumping and fumbling and grinding and awkwardness.

01 **Brand New** - Me vs. Maradona vs. Elvis
02 **Judas Priest** - Turbo Lover
03 **Peter Gabriel** - In Your Eyes
04 **Phil Collins** - In the Air Tonight
05 **Mazzy Starr** - Fade Into You
06 **Chris Isaak** - Wicked Game
07 **Marvin Gaye** - Let's Get It On
08 **Goldfrapp** - Black Cherry
09 **Beck** - Debra
10 **Sade** - By Your Side
11 **Lovage** - Strangers on a Train
12 **The Faint** - Worked Up So Sexual

13 **Barry White** - Can't Get Enough of Your
   Love, Babe
14 **Massive Attack** - Angel
15 **James** - Laid
16 **Nine Inch Nails** - Closer

## WAKE UP, SLEEPY FACE

Finding the energy to wake up in the morning can be hard. Most of us would prefer to bury our faces in our pillows for a few more hours. This mix starts off innocuously and then builds into an energized mix to help you get out of bed and on with your day.

01 **Karen O** - Hello Tomorrow
02 **Marc Bolan & T. Rex** - Cosmic Dancer
03 **The Velvet Underground** - Who Loves the Sun
04 **The Verve** - Velvet Morning
05 **Primal Scream** - Some Velvet Morning
06 **The Dandy Warhols** - Good Morning
07 **The Walkmen** - Wake Up
08 **The Mamas & the Papas** - Dream a Little Dream of Me
09 **The Partridge Family** - I Woke Up in Love This Morning
10 **The Polyphonic Spree** - It's the Sun
11 **Muse** - Sunburn
12 **Placebo** - Pure Morning
13 **Oasis** - Morning Glory
14 **No Doubt** - Sunday Morning

OTHER
PLAYLISTS

15 **Arcade Fire** - Wake Up
16 **Wham!** - Wake Me Up Before You Go-Go
17 **Ash** - A Life Less Ordinary
18 **Refused** - New Noise
19 **Supergrass** - Alright

OTHER
PLAYLISTS

## WALKING AROUND THE CITY ALONE

If the noisy sounds of garbage trucks, people screaming, and cars honking don't really appeal to you as a music fan, try pumping these songs through your headphones.

01 **Lenny Kravitz** - Let Love Rule
02 **The Libertines** - I Get Along
03 **Aerosmith** - Walk This Way
04 **Pet Shop Boys** - Suburbia
05 **Annie** - Chewing Gum
06 **Arcade Fire** - Neighborhood #3 (Power Out)
07 **Muse** - Time Is Running Out
08 **Interpol** - Evil
09 **Joy Division** - Transmission
10 **The Smiths** - Rubber Ring
11 **Scissor Sisters** - Take Your Mama
12 **R.E.M.** - Stand
13 **Cake** - The Distance
14 **David Bowie** - The Jean Genie
15 **The Beatles** - Twist and Shout
16 **The Rapture** - House of Jealous Lovers
17 **British Sea Power** - Blackout
18 **Blur** - Tender

19 **Moving Units** - Between Us & Them
20 **The Used** - The Taste of Ink
21 **The Jam** - Start!
22 **Brand New** - The Boy Who Blocked His
Own Shot
23 **Blondie** - Heart of Glass
24 **Iggy Pop** - Candy
25 **The Chemical Brothers** - Setting Sun
26 **Neil Diamond** - I'm a Believer
27 **The Clash** - Rock the Casbah
28 **Coldplay** - Yellow
29 **Wilco** - Can't Stand It
30 **The White Stripes** - Seven Nation Army

## WEDDING COCKTAIL HOUR

You're DJing a wedding, and it's cocktail hour. This is when you play songs that are a little more up-tempo than what you might play for the wedding dinner.

01 **Elton John** - Your Song
02 **The Jimi Hendrix Experience** - Little Wing
03 **Cyndi Lauper** - Time After Time
04 **The Cars** - Just What I Needed
05 **Stealers Wheel** - Stuck in the Middle With You
06 **Keane** - Somewhere Only We Know
07 **The Zombies** - Time of the Season
08 **Bonnie Tyler** - Total Eclipse of the Heart
09 **Siouxsie and the Banshees** - Kiss Them for Me
10 **Dusty Springfield** - Son of a Preacher Man
11 **Wham!** - Careless Whisper
12 **Tears for Fears** - Head Over Heels
13 **Oasis** - Live Forever
14 **Space** - Female of the Species
15 **Baby Bird** -You're Gorgeous

## WEDDING DINING MUSIC

Loud, garish music playing while people are trying to eat and chitchat can be really annoying. There's no use for it. Dinnertime is a great time to play lovely, light songs and jazz or orchestrated covers of popular songs. Why wait for a wedding to play this mix—invite some friends over, order some Chinese food, and press play!

01 **The Bad Plus** - Smells Like Teen Spirit
02 **SOC** - All Apologies
03 **Feist** - Leisure Suite
04 **The Sundays** - Wild Horses
05 **Fleetwood Mac** - Landslide
06 **Dido** - White Flag
07 **Ron Escheté** - Yesterday
08 **Steve Hulse** - Something
09 **Arthur Fiedler and the Boston Pops** - Hey Jude
10 **Christopher O'Riley** - You
11 **Christopher O'Riley** - True Love Waits
12 **The Righteous Brothers** - Unchained Melody
13 **The Postal Service** - Such Great Heights

OTHER PLAYLISTS

## WEDDING RECEPTION

There is really no joy better than DJing a wedding. Here you stand before a hundred or so people who are gathered for a really nice reason . . . and there's an open bar. So, basically, whatever you play will be totally loved by everyone there. You're going to want to play some slow songs toward the end of the night when people are really loaded and want to get up close and personal. But I'd like to suggest that you begin the night with things they all know. Here you go:

01 **a-ha** - Take On Me
02 **The B-52's** - Love Shack
03 **Blondie** - Atomic
04 **Bonnie Tyler** - Total Eclipse of the Heart
05 **The Cars** - Just What I Needed
06 **Chuck Berry** - You Never Can Tell
07 **Curtis Mayfield** - Superfly
08 **David Bowie** - Rebel Rebel
09 **Devo** - Girl U Want
10 **The Doors** - Love Street
11 **Dramarama** - Anything, Anything (I'll Give You)
12 **Elton John** - Your Song

OTHER
PLAYLISTS

13 **Elvis Presley** - Hound Dog
14 **Elvis Presley** - Can't Help Falling in Love
15 **Erasure** - A Little Respect
16 **The Lemonheads** - Into Your Arms
17 **Little Richard** - The Girl Can't Help It
18 **Louis Armstrong** - What a Wonderful World
19 **Muddy Waters** - Sugar Sweet
20 **Naked Eyes** - Always Something There to Remind Me
21 **Nat King Cole** - Unforgettable
22 **Pat Benatar** - Love Is a Battlefield
23 **Pixies** - Debaser
24 **The Postal Service** - Such Great Heights
25 **Pulp** - Do You Remember the First Time?
26 **Queen** - Another One Bites the Dust
27 **REO Speedwagon** - Keep On Loving You
28 **The Righteous Brothers** - Unchained Melody
29 **Sly & the Family Stone** - Family Affair
30 **Sly & the Family Stone** - Everyday People
31 **Stealers Wheel** - Stuck in the Middle with You
32 **Stevie Wonder** - Isn't She Lovely
33 **Styx** - Come Sail Away
34 **Tom Jones** - She's a Lady
35 **The Beatles** - Twist and Shout

OTHER PLAYLISTS

## YOU HAVE NO IDEA HOW MUCH I MISS YOU SO LET ME TELL YOU IN SONG

This list can be used in two ways:

1. You make it for the person you have a really obsessive crush on but don't know how to tell. (WARNING: You might very well scare this person away.)

2. You make it for the person you've broken up with and regret doing so because really, deep down, you love them and can't live your life without them—or at least haven't found someone better than them yet.

It can go either way, really. It's also just a really romantic mix that any person should feel very lucky to receive.

01 **Interpol** - Untitled
02 **Death Cab for Cutie** - Transatlanticism
03 **Joy Division** - Love Will Tear Us Apart
04 **Mazzy Star** - Fade Into You
05 **The Cure** - Lovesong
06 **Nada Surf** - Inside of Love
07 **Beck** - Lost Cause
08 **Blur** - Out of Time

09 **Calla** - Strangler

10 **Morrissey** - Whatever Happens, I Love You

11 **INXS** - Never Tear Us Apart

12 **Yeah Yeah Yeahs** - Maps

13 **The Smiths** - Asleep

14 **Nirvana** - Something in the Way

15 **The Runaways** - Wait for Me

16 **The Oohlas** - Gone

17 **Rival Schools** - Undercovers On

18 **Placebo** - My Sweet Prince

19 **Travis** - As You Are

20 **The Beach Boys** - God Only Knows (Stereo Mix)

21 **Broken Social Scene** - Lover's Spit

22 **Cyndi Lauper** - When You Were Mine

**OTHER PLAYLISTS**

## YOU'RE BETTER OFF WITHOUT HIM/HER

There's this moment right after a friend's breakup when you need to intercept them and remind them what a horrible person they were dating. This time is vital. They will start to remember all the nice stuff and call their ex and grovel, and you can't let that happen! Here are some songs to help them remember the bad parts, but in a way that won't hurt so much.

01 **Franz Ferdinand** - Cheating on You
02 **The Libertines** - Can't Stand Me Now
03 **Pat Benatar** - Love Is a Battlefield
04 **Aaliyah** - Try Again
05 **Ace of Base** - The Sign
06 **Paula Abdul** - Cold Hearted
07 **Christina Aguilera** - What a Girl Wants
08 **Asia** - Heat of the Moment
09 **Backstreet Boys** - Quit Playing Games (With My Heart)
10 **Baha Men** - Who Let the Dogs Out
11 **Gloria Gaynor** - I Will Survive
12 **Duran Duran** - Come Undone

# DIGITAL MUSIC PLAYERS

Chances are, by the time you read this you will be able to buy an MP3 player that holds up to a million songs and is the size of a matchbook.

## APPLE iPOD (MAC OR PC)

Apple has several different sizes of iPods that can be broken down into four categories:

**iPod Shuffle:** Holds only between 120 and 240 songs and only has a shuffle function. It doesn't have a display, so you can't search for songs. You just have to wait and hope it comes on.

**iPod Mini:** Holds about six gigs of music, which is about a thousand songs.

**Standard iPod:** Can hold between twenty and sixty gigs of music. It's the standard device for good reason: It's easy to use, reliable, and nicely designed.

**iPod Photo:** This allows you to store not only music, but also photos, which can be viewed on the display screen of the iPod, on a computer via a USB cable, or on a TV via an AV cable.

## CREATIVE ZEN MICRO

Similar to the iPod Mini, it has a larger capacity, can play not only MP3s but also WMA files, *and* it has an FM radio transmitter.

## SAMSUNG YEPP YP-T5 V

This incredibly small and nearly weightless digital music player is available for under one hundred dollars and could fit in your front pocket with minimal bulk (though I know you'll be happy to see me). Unlike the similarly sized iPod Shuffle, this has a display screen.

## iRIVER H140

Holds up to forty gigs of music and comes with a voice/audio recorder as well as an FM radio. The sound quality is pretty superb.

## DELL POCKET DJ

This affordable five-gig DMP is lightweight and affordable. Plays MP3 and WMA files.

# WHERE TO DOWNLOAD MUSIC

## PAY SITES

iTunes.com (Windows/Mac)

Napster (www.napster.com) (Windows)

Rhapsody (www.listen.com) (Windows)

Walmart.com (Windows/Mac)

Emusic.com (Windows/Mac)

## PEER-TO-PEER SITES

These are free, peer-to-peer file-sharing programs that allow users to share any digital file including images, audio, video, and software. These are by no means legal, may contain viruses, and are unreliable.

SoulSeek (www.download-it-free.com/soulseek) (Windows)

Kazaa (www.kazaa.com) (Windows)

BitTorrent (www.bittorrent.com) (Windows/Mac)

LimeWire (www.limewire.com) (Windows/Mac)

Ares (www.aresgalaxy.org) (Windows)

WinMX (www.winmx.com) (Windows)
BearShare (www.bearshare.com) (Windows)
SoulseeX (chris.schleifer.net/ssX) (Mac)

## WEBLOGS

Weblogs are personal Web sites. Here are some
to check out, along with what you'll find there:

Chips & Cookies (chipsandcookies.blogspot.com)
  (full albums)
Cocaineblunts.com (hip hop)
Copy, right? (copycommaright.blogspot.com)
  (covers)
Coverville.com (covers)
Fluxblog.org (indie-rock hits before they hit)
The Hype Machine (hype.non-standard.net)
  (archive of blogger-posted MP3s)
Largehearted boy (blog.largeheartedboy.com)
  (only does legal and live stuff)
Scenestars.net (indie)
*Sixeyes (sixeyes.blogspot.com) (indie)
Stereogum.com (indie and some pop stuff)

# FUN GADGETS!

## iTRIP FM TRANSMITTER (WORKS WITH iPOD)

This is great for anyone who wants to listen to the songs on their DMP on their car stereo or anywhere where there's a radio. Basically, the device picks up the signal of your player and transmits it to the radio, where you can listen to it on a designated station. The only problem is that sometimes the radio signal is weak, making it hard to hear what's playing, which can be frustrating.

## CAR CASSETTE ADAPTER (WORKS WITH ALL MP3 PLAYERS)

Just like the above, this device allows you to listen to your DMP through your car stereo. I find it to be more reliable because you don't have to worry about picking up a radio signal, but you do need to worry about having a tape player in your car, which is more rare these days.

EXTRAS

## iBEAM LASER POINTER AND FLASHLIGHT (WORKS WITH iPODS)

This is one of the most pointless accessories you could have: It's a flashlight adaptor that plugs into your iPod.

## POD WAVE PORTABLE STEREO SPEAKER (WORKS WITH iPODS)

This plugs into your iPod and allows you to listen to your songs out loud so you can annoy everyone on the subway, bus, etc.

## naviPOD WIRELESS REMOTE CONTROL (WORKS WITH iPODS)

If you have your DMP hooked up to your stereo, you'll notice that the slightly annoying thing is having to get up from wherever you're sitting whenever a song you're not into comes on. This remote control will save you the trip.

## inMOTION PORTABLE AUDIO SYSTEM (WORKS WITH iPODS)

Designed exclusively for the iPod, the ultra-portable Altec Lansing inMotion audio system (with built-in dock) provides outstanding sound in a highly portable size.

## BATTERY PACK (WORKS WITH iPODS)

This plugs into your iPod and gives it added life.

EXTRAS

 **Sarah Lewitinn**, also known as Ultragrrrl, is a former writer and editor at *Spin* magazine and a sought after DJ. In addition to having her own A&R company, Sarah keeps a popular blog in which she chronicles the current music scene and documents her party life. She appears regularly as a "talking head" on VH1, E!, CNN, and Fox, and lives in New York City.

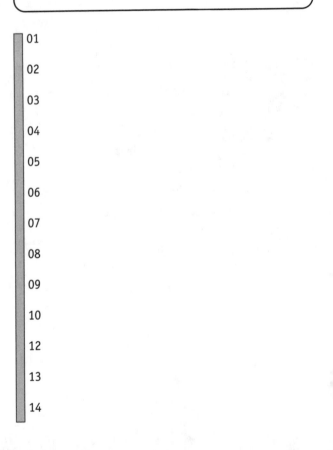

01

02

03

04

05

06

07

08

09

10

12

13

14

15
16
17
18
19
20
21
22
23
24
25
26
27
28
29
30

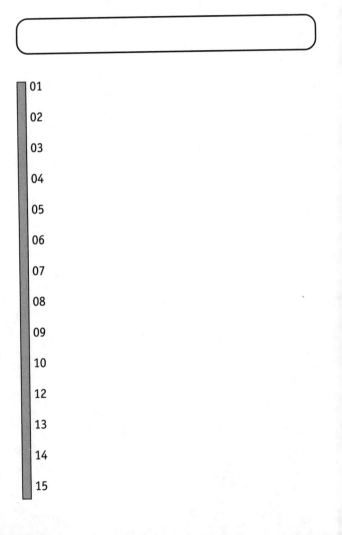

01

02

03

04

05

06

07

08

09

10

12

13

14

15